Praise for *Chasing the North Wind* and the Krotz family legacy.

"The Krotz family story exemplifies the independent spirit shared by the people of Cook County. Clarence Krotz followed his dreams to the shores of Devil Track Lake, and with determination and hard work brought them to life. In memories shared by Clarence's daughter, Kathy Krotz-Finn—a free spirit with her own love of soaring above lakes and forests—Richard Struck reveals the legacy of aviation in this region."

—*Carrie Johnson, Former Executive Director*
Cook County Historical Society

"Richard Struck and Kathy Krotz-Finn have written a wonderful, historically accurate account of the development of an airport, aviation, and its part in the growth of tourism in Cook County. An enjoyable and educational read for locals, the thousands of tourists who visit each year, and people around the country who are interested in the history of aviation."

—*Eugene Glader, Ph.D. Former College Professor*
Author of "Downtown Grand Marais," Volumes 1 and 2

"Kathy's story is a great example of the grand old days of northern Minnesota flying. The local history and aviation family stories are fun and bring the charm and lore of early Cook County back to life. Every pilot would love to have grown up with those memories and flying experiences."

—*Mike Raymond,*
Owner of Red Pine Realty
Certified Flight Instructor

"We are inspired by and thankful for the Krotz family's foundational work in establishing aviation in Cook County. It is fitting that our modern facility is located on Krotz land. We hope that this history of Cook County aviation and Kathy's example reach the minds and imaginations of our citizens and visitors, especially our young men and women—the future of aviation."

—*John Barton, Lt. Col., USAF (ret)*
Chairman, Grand Marais/Cook County Airport Commission
Certified Flight Instructor

"A must-read that brings the Krotz family history to life! This story is an inspiration. Learn about the family's challenges and celebrations while running a northwoods lodge, airport, and seaplane base in the late 1940s in northern Minnesota. We're honored to continue the legacy of celebrating aviation history here."

—*Rachelle and Cory Christianson, Owners*
Skyport Lodge and Resort,
Devil Track Lake, Minnesota

"The legacy of a fellow veteran, 1st Lieutenant Clarence J. Krotz of the U.S. Army Air Corps, is alive today through his family and the story of the three daughters who became "flying sisters" on the airport their father built. Lt. Krotz's restored J-3 Cub flies today with daughter Kathy at the controls. Now over 70 years of age, she is an inspiration.

"As Kathy shows, flying never seems to get old or routine. Each flight is interesting and exciting. It builds confidence and skill. Safety, attention to detail, maneuvers, emergency procedures, and navigation all become second nature. Take a ride with an instructor to experience flight. Handle the controls. You might get hooked. You are never too young or too old to try something new."

—*Robert Mordini, Ph.D.,*
Former College Professor, Pilot

"[This] book is both of local interest and national importance in that [it] relates a story that is fairly uncommon in the aviation world—an industry that has only recently seen women in reasonable numbers. Kathy's story—notable in a time period that makes her rare indeed—needs to be told."

—*Rodney Roy, Pilot*
Manager, Fixed Base Operations Grand Marais Airport
Vintage Aircraft Restoration Expert

"I love the story of the Piper Pilot up north… What a woman!"

—*Curt Brown, Freelance Writer*
Minneapolis Star Tribune
Minnesota History

"*Chasing the North Wind* paints a well-deserved image of Kathy Krotz-Finn, an exceptional woman [with a] lifelong love affair with aviation. Who can resist a well-told story of flying a J-3 Cub by a person from the Boundary Waters region? A must-read for those with an interest in Minnesota's rich aviation history. I know that the Minnesota Pilots Association members will relish the tales of this woman flying in what still remains quite a wilderness."

—*Randy Corfman, President*
Minnesota Pilots Association

"Kathy's book, *Chasing the North Wind,* brings back many fond memories of aviation's early influence in our lives. My earliest memories of Skyport Lodge, Kathy's girlhood home so many years ago, occurred in the mid-60s, when, for less than a dollar, my friends and I would board a bus at school and head to 'the lake.' Whether on or off the water, Devil Track Lake was always 'buzzing' with boat and plane activity.

"My aunt and uncle owned a cabin that was just west of the old airport runway. The takeoffs and landings were always exciting as it seemed you could almost reach out and touch the planes. As good fortune would have it, I now live on the north side of Devil Track Lake and am able to watch the seaplanes take off and land all summer long. I even enjoy watching jet aircraft today using our new airport just north of Devil Track Lake. In this way the Skyport legacy continues to support Cook County."

—*Linda Jurek, Executive Director*
Visit Cook County Minnesota

"I am very proud of and grateful to my sister, Kathy, for many reasons. One of the most important is her commitment to our father's memory by restoring our family's J-3 Piper Cub, keeping it aloft, and flying again at the age of 70. A lot of sacrifices were made during her life to carry on the legacy of the Krotz family flying service. Commitment, determination, and a love of flying have influenced her desire to be an inspiration to other women of all ages to follow their dreams to achieve anything and everything possible."

—*Ginger Krotz-Berglund*
Krotz Family Historian

Chasing the North Wind

A Memoir of One Woman's Lifelong Love Affair Flying a Vintage 1941 Piper J-3 Cub Aircraft and Growing Up in Minnesota's Famed Arrowhead Region

—

By Kathryn Krotz-Finn
With Richard C. Struck
Foreword by Wolfgang Greiner
Edited by Rose Arrowsmith

Kathryn Krotz Finn

*Sincere appreciation is given to
Wolfgang Greiner for his encouragement, support,
and a charitable grant from the Wolfgang Charitable Trust
for the partnership with the Cook County Historical Society
and the Grand Marais State Bank,
in making this book possible.*

Copyright 2023
All Rights Reserved

ISBN: 979-8-218-25772-9

Printed in the United States

10 9 8 7 6 5 4 3 2

Produced By
Northern Wilds Media, Inc.
Grand Marais, MN
www.northernwilds.com

*Dedicated to my parents,
Clarence and Dorothy Krotz,
whose guidance and support gave me
both the confidence to fly, and the gift
of real wings to fulfill my dreams.
And to my sisters Ginger and Clarice whose
loving support throughout our lives together
helped me chase the wind.*

VIII | CHASING THE NORTH WIND

FOREWORD

I have always had a love for flying, the north country, its history, and the people that make their homes in this beautiful land of endless forests and countless lakes.

I started flying back when mowing lawns and shoveling snow earned enough to pay for flying lessons. Today, it takes a bit more money, but no more passion or interest, to join those adventurers who need to see the earth from above or dance around a big white cloud on a summer afternoon.

There is something magical about the far off drone of an airplane coming over the horizon or soaring into the sunset. From the Gulf of Mexico to Hudson Bay, on to the Arctic Ocean and west to Alaska, at airports, seaplane bases, and outpost camps, whenever I land my red and white Aviat Husky floatplane, friendly people stop to chat, share a cup of coffee, and "check out the airplane."

The moment I met Kathryn Krotz-Finn and we started talking about flying, I knew we were kindred souls. Her smile and the sparkle in her eyes as she shared many stories about growing up at a wilderness seaplane base said it all. In this book, Kathryn weaves together the story of her father Clarence Krotz, a WWII bomber pilot, and the Krotz family as they build a seaplane base and resort on Devil Track Lake in northern Minnesota. Clarence taught all three of his teenage daughters to fly back when "girls did not fly airplanes." It's fitting that these stories of Kathryn's remarkable upbringing and lifelong love of the magic of flight are set to a backdrop of endless miles of pristine wilderness.

More than a Cook County history lesson, we learn about the people that settled this rugged land, about airplanes and the joy of flying, and how a small gravel runway and seaplane dock have grown into a robust airport that serves as a gateway to the Arrowhead region.

Join me in exploring a lifetime of adventure in the air with Kathryn and her yellow Piper Cub.

—Wolfgang Greiner

PREFACE

The idea for this story came about from a chance meeting with Kathryn Krotz-Finn at the Grand Marais State Bank a few years back. In our brief chat, Kathryn casually said she owned a vintage 1941 Piper J-3 Cub aircraft. As a small plane enthusiast with a lifelong interest in aviation, I had to know more about Kathryn and her Cub.

We met over coffee in a small meeting room at the local co-op. I brought with me a list of basic questions on her background, the Cub, and her family. She answered each one with enthusiasm. I was drawn in at once by her quiet manner, humor, and warm style, and I knew readers would be, too. She was open to my suggestion that her story was a good one, and we agreed to try to develop her memoir for possible publication. This book is the outcome of our work together, supplemented with research support from the helpful staff of the Cook County Historical Society and the Grand Marais Public Library.

Kathryn is a wonderful role model for women with an interest in aviation; our community is extremely fortunate to have her, and other pilots and flight-minded folks.

We hope you enjoy her story.

—Richard C. Struck

XII | CHASING THE NORTH WIND

ACKNOWLEDGEMENTS

I was born into a family dedicated to the gift of flight. With a father trained in WWII as a bomber pilot, and a mother of many talents and considerable patience, I found aviation early in my life. Even as a girl, to have this experience was considered natural, and my parents encouraged me and my sisters every step of the way, especially to learn to fly. And thanks to them, I inherited the vintage J-3 Piper Cub.

My sisters, Ginger and Clarice, made this aviation story a good one. Their constant encouragement, good humor, and patience helped me know that the Cub would one day become a major part of my life. Clarice died in January 2019 after a long illness. Ginger's keen mind and a talent for recollecting key facts of our lives added greatly to this story. We had lots of just plain fun recalling the good old days. And now our children and grandchildren can enjoy our story as well.

My husband, Doug, took lessons when he was young, soloed when living up on the Iron Range, started a family, and then stopped flying. Although not a licensed pilot, he continues to offer constant encouragement and support for my flying, and the courage to write my story. Thus, while caring for several foster children over the years, running a house, managing a large garden, helping maintain our rural homestead, and even working in town, I managed to keep the flying "bug" alive. I could not have done this without his loving support.

Maintaining an aircraft requires mechanical skills of many kinds. My good friend Russell Smith stepped forward following my dad's death and offered to help me rebuild the J-3 Cub. Russ is also a good pilot, and we've enjoyed many flights together. His son, David, also a pilot, continues this support today and he's just like his dad—always cheerful and helpful.

Rodney Roy, manager of the Fixed Base Operations of the Grand Marais Airport, also played a major role in keeping the Cub up to snuff. Rod replaced the main wood wing spars and did other tasks to make the Cub airworthy. His expertise with old planes is nationally recognized, as he is considered an expert in vintage aircraft restoration.

To have Rod's hand in servicing the Cub only adds to its incredible value and airworthiness.

I am also grateful to the following folks whose interest, support, and encouragement brings the story of aviation in Cook County alive: Marja Erickson, Board President, Cook County Historical Society; Eugene Glader, Ph.D., author of two books on the history of Grand Marais; Mike Raymond, Certified Flight Instructor; John Barton, Lt.Col. USAF, (ret), Chairman, Grand Marais/Cook County Airport Commission Board; Rachelle and Cory Christianson, Owners, Skyport Lodge; Robert Mordini, Ph.D., pilot and plane owner; Linda Jurek, Executive Director, Visit Cook County Minnesota; and Randy Corfman, President, Minnesota Pilots Association. An extra thanks is also given to Curt Brown, feature writer for the Minneapolis *Star Tribune* who ran my story in the *Star Tribune,* August 4, 2019.

I wish to point out the special support of Wolfgang Greiner, local resident, pilot, and former business executive, whose charitable grant to the Cook County Historical Society forged this partnership to publish my book.

To have a written memoir to tell my particular story, and that of the Krotz family, is an awesome achievement and a wonderful gift. For this I owe considerable thanks to Richard Struck who offered to write our story.

As I'm now over 70 years old, I pray for continued good health, an aircraft that will continue to fulfill my dreams, and good air to keep me aloft. Thanks for sharing this journey with me, and safe flying. And to my friends and all those who might be considering the beauty and joy of flight, I say, don't wait to try it.

—**Kathryn Krotz-Finn**

INTRODUCTION

As a girl growing up in the late 1940s at a lodge and airport in the semi-wilderness of northeastern Minnesota, my life's experiences have been shaped by airplanes and the allure of traveling aloft on fabric wings, dancing on air with the birds and clouds to keep me company. This life was possible thanks to my parents, Clarence and Dorothy Krotz, whose commitment to aviation and unwavering support for me and my two sisters kept us growing in many ways.

My story is made up of three major influences that truly molded and continue to influence my life. Neither segment is meant to be a complete overview, but I hope enough to show you how my life and outlook were formed. Simply stated, our lives were uniquely different from most folks living nearby.

The first element of the story is that of our father coming to Cook County after he was discharged from the U.S. Army Air Corps in 1945, buying property, marrying our mother, and starting construction on what was to become Skyport Lodge and airport, the first successful enterprise of its kind in the county. This new business reflected and encouraged the early growth of general aviation in the Arrowhead region. In this way my book is also a tribute to my father.

The second part of my life is growing up at the lodge with my two sisters, Ginger and Clarice. While our folks struggled to develop the lodge and airfield, we girls pitched in to help wherever and whenever we could to make ends meet. As we grew, there was no task we wouldn't attempt, and in time our support was a key to the financial success of Skyport Lodge and airport. Our folks welcomed this help and, in turn, Dad gave each of us flying lessons. Although we all soloed successfully, I was the only sister who wanted to obtain a pilot's license, which I still have.

The third part of this story is that of my adult life and how the allure of aviation stayed with me in spite of the challenges of married life, raising children, and helping our parents in their later years. During my first two marriages and the time following my dad's death, my flying enthusiasm often waned when I was confronted by the absence of Dad's support, the demands of children, including foster kids, home and income needs, and especially husbands lacking any interest in flying or aviation generally. Now, my third and current husband, Doug, is entirely supportive of my passion for flight, and this makes all the difference.

Another story to tell is of aviation in Cook County. In 2023 Cook County residents celebrate 75 years of aviation (1948–2023). My story and this book help describe this achievement, an important milestone in transportation, recreation, and the value and beauty of flight.

It is with great humility that I have compiled this story, at times including or reflecting essays published in the *Cook County News Herald,* articles I've submitted for publication to other news outlets, and materials I've used to speak with Rotary members and other groups. I've often said, as an adult, that I wish I could go back and talk with my parents about their interests and values, and what shaped them into the people they became. Perhaps this material will help my family and friends better understand what was important in my life.

I'm often asked, why would a young woman or anyone want to fly? Well, I fly for the same reason Amelia Earhart flew: "For the fun of it!" Similarly, there is an old saying: "There is a book to be written about everyone's life." Here is mine.

Table of Contents

IX Foreword, by Wolfgang Greiner

XI Preface, by Richard C. Struck

XIII Acknowledgements

XV Introduction

PROLOGUE: First Flight of Spring. 1

CHAPTER 1: Lure of the Wanderlust 5

CHAPTER 2: Stick-to-it-ive-ness 9

CHAPTER 3: Getting Our Wings 15

CHAPTER 4: Childhood Adventures 21

CHAPTER 5: The Family Business. 29

CHAPTER 6: Family of Fliers 33

CHAPTER 7: Flight Notes 39

CHAPTER 8: Learning to Fly 43

CHAPTER 9: Rite of Passage 47

CHAPTER 10: New Horizons 51

CHAPTER 11: Long-Awaited Dreams 55

CHAPTER 12: Grounded 59

CHAPTER 13: Aloft Again 63

CHAPTER 14: Hangar Flying 65

EPILOGUE: Chasing the North Wind. 69

Postscript 73

An Invitation for Women Pilots 75

Aircraft & Aviation Terms: Piper J-3 Cub 77

Profile of Clarence J. Krotz 79

History of the Grand Marais Airport 81

Floats or Wheels 83

Airport Statistics 1947-1965 85

Cook County Aviation Quiz 87

Timeline 89

Selected Bibliography 93

Author Biographies 94

PROLOGUE:

First Flight of Spring

I have always been impatient for the first flight of spring, like a kid waiting for Christmas to arrive. To paraphrase an old saying from Robert Louis Stevenson, 'I don't fly to go anywhere, but to go!' Whether it's a mere circle of 50 miles or a longer flight, just to be airborne is pure joy, even after my six decades aloft.

This year's first May flight, like so many before it, begins with the simple act of circling a Saturday on my calendar. To my great pleasure, the morning dawns brightly as the eastern sun graces tree tops that are just showing the slight green of new buds. The comfortable 50-degree temperature, low breezes from the southwest, and clear, robin's egg blue skies all signal a delightful beginning for another season of flying in my 1941 Piper J-3 Cub.

It is 7:00 a.m. when I arrive at Devil Track Lake where I keep the Cub. The lake is calm and I am pleased that I'm alone. Well, almost alone. The occasional liquid notes of the robin and the chuck-chuck of the red-winged blackbird greet me. Chickadees, nuthatches, and blue jays busily search for their morning food, and their antics are welcome company. Though I don't hear their calls, I know Minnesota's state bird, the common loon, has already arrived to stake out early, ice-free waters on which to raise its young. As author Sigurd F. Olson said, the cry of the loon epitomizes the northern wilderness.

Who knows what I might see below me once I'm up in the air? With the Cub's relatively slow airspeed, some patches of snow still on the ground, and little leaf cover, most creatures moving about below me will be fairly easy to spot. It has always been a thrill to note how many sightings I can log on each flight, and I have often traced the activity of wolves, moose, and deer in the boreal forest far below.

The long-cherished aroma of pine trees and warming forest grasses embraces me as I begin my traditional pre-flight checks. I don't recall how many hundreds of times I've done this in my life, but it's a ritual that never loses its appeal. After so many years I can do it by memory, yet as my life depends on a thorough and careful check of the plane for both safety and good overall performance, I never rush this process.

I walk around the Cub checking the elevators, rudder, and ailerons to make sure they're moving correctly. Then I check the engine oil, make sure there was no water in the fuel, and check the pitot tube, which indicates air speed. Next, I run my hand over the leading edges of the wings and over the body of the plane to see if the heavy duty Seconite fabric is damaged in any way.

Though I've always been grateful that the Cub's snow skis have exempted me from cabin-bound winters, I love the Cub best with floats on, and I have already eagerly swapped out the skis for floats and now make sure no water has seeped into them.

A full gas tank allows for only two hours of flight time, but as I am not rushed, I plan to make an extended loop to the west and then back to Grand Marais, meandering about 50 or so land miles. This will take me over Devil Track Lake, Ball Club Lake, Two Island Lake, and many other smaller lakes and streams that feed into Lake Superior.

If my flight plan were longer, or if winds were out of the north, it would be necessary to check official weather predictions and file a flight plan, even though I fly by Visual Flight Rules only. But for this short flight I can trust in the motto I learned from my dad years ago: "If the birds don't fly, neither do I;" and in the knowledge that my husband, Doug, would come looking for me if I didn't return as scheduled.

With the time-honored checklist complete, I am ready to take to the skies!

The Cub is a working plane, and often a favorite of bush pilots around the world. Even when parked, it shouts its natural beauty and simplicity. Contrary to modern aircraft with their array of sophisticated instruments and complex controls, starting a Cub is easy. I set the throttle, pull the magnetos to the "on" position, then move to the front of the plane via the right float. Before I give the propeller a good fast turn with one hand, I holler "switch is on... contact," even though no one else is around. Dad always drummed this into me and my sisters when giving us flight training. The engine starts and I immediately pull my hand away from the turning prop, and feel the rush of adrenaline that always responds to the sound of the engine and the faint odor of oil and fuel. I keep the engine running and shut off one magneto at a time, ensuring there is only a slight drop in revolutions per minute.

Next, I untie the floats and give a slight nudge away from the dock as I jump onto the float. As the 65-hp Continental engine warms up with its deep, familiar cadence, I climb into the Cub. I sit in the back as I always do for proper load balancing when flying solo, and close the lower half of the entry door. I leave the upper portion open so I can feel and smell the cool spring air once aloft. Although the interior of the Cub is not insulated, I never usually wear a cap or scarf like other pilots, except during the deep cold of winter. Perhaps that can be chalked up to vanity, but on this beautiful May day I am comfortable in my usual outfit of jeans and a sweater, a wool jacket, heavy socks, a good pair of hiking boots, and gloves.

You might not believe me when I say the Cub and I are bonded after all our years together, but I can feel that it wants to fly as much as I do. I can sense the power and anticipation! I instinctively reach for the round knob of the throttle lever mounted just under the window on my left. My right hand holds the control stick between my legs. With both feet on the rudder pedals, I slowly move the throttle lever forward. The trick now is to control both throttle and rudder to keep moving in a straight line. I check the magnetos, instruments, rudder pedals, ailerons, and control stick once more. I also look again for people in boats who might be quite surprised to see a float plane roaring toward them across the lake surface, or birds who might cause a low-altitude collision.

All clear for take-off!

After a long winter of waiting for this moment, it's time to go. I firmly ease the throttle forward and the Cub's engine comes to life with its loud, distinctive purr..r..r.! Instantly, the familiar power of this good engine, the vibrations surrounding me in my small cockpit, and the sound of the floats skimming the water's surface below reassure and excite me.

The Cub is a light plane and soon reaches the desired take-off speed of 58 mph. I pull back lightly on the stick to raise the Cub's nose, the floats leave the water, and the plane begins to climb. I lower the nose slightly to gain air speed and then resume the climb until I reach my desired altitude. At full throttle, the engine steadily pulls me upward into the wonderful western blue sky. I check my instruments again: altimeter, tachometer, airspeed indicator, and engine temperature gauge. Everything is just as it should be, so with a slight push forward on the control stick, I begin level flight and the start of another morning of pure flying adventure.

What could be nicer to celebrate the new spring season? At 2,000 feet I pull the throttle back for a level cruising speed of 58 mph, settle back for my flight and relaxed my grip on the stick. With the morning sun at my back and the waves of Lake Superior glistening on my left, I feel as light as a feather. I am back in touch with my friend the sky.

Though Helen Keller wasn't actually describing flying, she surely could have been when she said, "For one wild, glad moment we snapped the chain that binds us to earth, and joining hands with the winds we felt ourselves divine."

CHAPTER 1:

Lure of the Wanderlust

"Lure of the Wanderlust" Attracts Tourists...
the road from Duluth to Port Arthur is one that rain or wind does not spoil—a fine graveled highway that leads on and on through whispering pines and sighing birches, over murmuring streams with speckled beauties and past wonderful waterfalls. No wonder Grand Marais is bound to become one of the greatest summer resorts, waiting to be discovered in order to be enjoyed."

—*Grand Marais News Herald,* July 19, 1919

Growing up in Cook County is a cherished part of my life; it's the only place I want to be, and for good reason. Here in the Arrowhead Region of the Superior National Forest, there's a lot to be proud of. The "inland sea" of Lake Superior has half of the volume of all the Great Lakes combined, and it holds ten percent of the world's fresh water. The town of Grand Marais sits nestled on its shore, with the famously tranquil Boundary Waters Canoe Area Wilderness just up over the hill a ways. It's no surprise that thousands of visitors each year journey north to see it for themselves.

But in the early 1900s, getting here was simply beyond the reach of most folks. As there was no rail line from Duluth or Canada, nor any land-based airports, residents and visitors made the journey by boat, sled dog, or primitive roads. Only the very hardy took up the challenge. You could say the romance and practicality of flight was a marriage waiting to happen. Indeed, it was only a matter of time before the lure of the north and advancements in air travel spurred growth in both transportation and the economic outlook for the County.

In 1913, one of the first aircraft in our area was shipped from St. Louis, MO, to Duluth: a Benoit XIV No. 43 bi-plane "flying boat."

In 1919, the U.S. Army announced that army aircraft would begin to fight forest fires to protect the national forests. This offered a valuable opportunity for training fliers and further developing the purposes and uses of aircraft, and the art of flying.

In August 1928, Frank and Will Powell of Gunflint Lake purchased a hydroplane, one of the first privately owned aircraft in

Clarence J. Krotz, circa 1940.

the county. The following winter, a tri-motored Ford plane on skis landed on the frozen Grand Marais harbor ice and gave about 300 county residents their first airplane ride. You can be sure that was a memorable winter.

But the real change began in 1933 when Grand Marais mayor J. Henry Eliasen was invited to discuss a possible airport facility in conjunction with the Works Progress Administration (WPA) of the Department of Commerce. Without an airstrip on land, primitive aircraft could only visit Cook County if they were equipped with floats or skis. Previously, the only landing field in Grand Marais was a stretch of old US 61, located north of town, with two runways, no hangars, and limited service. The WPA program was to help establish and improve airports for 2,000 villages in the country and to boost employment during the nation's depression period. A grant of $12,000 was discussed for Grand Marais, mainly for labor to build an airport runway 3,000 feet long and 550 feet wide. On December 20, 1933, 63 workers took up the task on what is today the Cook County High School football field.

Three years later, on July 23, 1936, the airstrip received the first-ever plane to land on Cook County soil: the U.S. Army Douglas monoplane piloted by Captain A.W. Nelson. Captain Nelson was on an inspection tour of Minnesota airports under the WPA program, and his inspection indicated that much was still necessary to bring the airport up to requirements.

With airport construction now underway, former Cook County Sheriff Emerson Morris became one of the early private plane owners by purchasing a Taylor Cub in 1940. As an army veteran, Morris joined a growing migration of servicemen and former military pilots into Cook County following the end of WWII, including my father, **Clarence J. Krotz.**

My father's arrival in Cook County in 1945 was actually a historic event. Although unknown and unheralded, he brought with him a dream that had helped sustain him during the war. That dream would impact the county and significantly influence the growth of aviation in northeastern Minnesota.

Dad was born May 16, 1920 in Chicago and began his active military service on May 24, 1943. First Lieutenant Krotz was a B-26 Lockheed Martin Marauder Bomber pilot and a member of the 432nd Bomber Squadron operating in the Mediterranean Theater of Operations, originally called the North African Theater of Operations covering North Africa and Italy during WWII.

Flying the B-26 was not easy. It was designed as a high-speed medium bomber for close ground tactical support. Powered by two, 2,000-hp Pratt & Whitney R-2800-43 Double Wasp piston engines, it had a maximum speed of 283 mph, a ceiling of 19,800 feet, and a range of 1,100 miles. The plane had a crew of seven. Only the most experienced pilots could comfortably handle the plane. The combat career of this plane began in the Pacific but it achieved its main successes in Europe and North Africa. Later models of the Marauder had as many turret guns as the Boeing B-17 Flying Fortress, and as many fixed guns as some fighter aircraft. It carried a normal bomb load of 3,000 pounds.

My father saw action in Sardinia, Italy, North Africa and the European Theater. After safely completing a stunning total of 72 missions, Dad's fellow pilots called him the "golden boy" for always returning without damage to his aircraft or injury to the crew. This changed drastically, however, on his 73rd and final mission when an enemy cannon shell tore through the bottom of his plane's nose, destroyed Dad's pilot seat, and killed his co-pilot. When he was discharged from active duty on October 7, 1945 at the young age of 25, he received two Bronze Stars, EAME Campaign Medal, Presidential Unit Citation with one Oak Leaf Cluster, and the Air Medal with five Oak Leaf Clusters.

In spite of constant danger during this high-risk service, he had kept his thoughts on another challenge and a major lifestyle change, should he survive the war. He wanted to combine his love of flying with his passion for the outdoors. In this he envisioned the ideal resort: a combination northwoods lodge-airport-seaplane base somewhere in north central Minnesota, and Cook County was just the place to make his dream a reality.

CHAPTER 2:

Stick-to-it-ive-ness

With his war time savings, Dad purchased a lodge and 77.6 acres of land on Devil Track Lake from Ronald Bent for the sum of $8,000. It lay along the north shore of the lake, extending inland to the north to include the land where the present-day airport is located. The deed for the land purchase was recorded in the Cook County court house on August 15, 1946. At that time, all appeared in order.

But our family's livelihood nearly came to an abrupt end almost as soon as it had begun. Shortly after the purchase was complete, Cook County officials informed Dad of an error in the land survey and told him he now owned only a portion of the bottom of Devil Track Lake. He was shocked! If he wanted to purchase the land he thought he had just acquired, he would have to pay the county an additional $8,000. This required securing another loan from the Grand Marais State Bank to buy the property a second time. That amount of money in those days was no small thing and only added to the stresses already confronting him. Yet Dad was a fighter and he knew he had to keep his energy and work focused. He showed some real Norwegian "sagleva," the "stick-to-it-ive-ness" our family, and so many northern folks, value highly.

1946
Lodge and acreage purchased on Devil Track Lake AUGUST 15

1947
Skyport Airfield constructed

1948
Airport and seaplane base license issued OCTOBER 9

Grand Marais airport granted limited license

State of MN purchased Skyport airfield for $10,000

Skyport officially the county airfield NOVEMBER 11

1949
Wilderness aircraft ban (IN EFFECT JANUARY 1951/1952)

1950
Purchase of 1941 Piper J-3 Cub

1954
Skyport Airport incorporated IN JUNE

1959
Tri-Pacer Cub purchased

Skyport Lodge 1950s.

In 1947 Dad began designing and building the airport later called Skyport airfield. His plans for a fly-in resort and campground would follow as funds allowed.

I imagine it felt pretty good when he was highlighted in the April 1, 1948 edition of the *Cook County News Herald's* feature, "Who's Who in North Shore Aviation."

The concept of aviation in Cook County was now an accepted fact that was eagerly promoted by civic leaders such as J. Henry Eliasen, mayor of Grand Marais; A. G. Porter, President, Lutsen Light and Power Co.; A. M. Anderson, President, Grand Marais State Bank; John Ruan, owner of Ruan Trucking Company; and John Skoglund, major partner in North Central Airlines Company.

In the spring of 1948, the *Cook County News Herald* ran feature stories entitled, "Who's Who in North Shore Aviation." In addition to stories featuring J. Henry Eliasen, A. G. Porter and A. M. Anderson, our dad Clarence J. Krotz was featured in the April 1, 1948 edition.

CHAPTER 2: STICK-TO-IT-IVE-NESS | 11

A state inspector inspected the unfinished airport built by our dad on Devil Track Lake and found everything in order and being properly constructed. To Dad's delight, a license was issued on the spot before he had actually completed the airport. License No. 518 dated October 9, 1948 was issued to Clarence J. Krotz to operate an airport and seaplane base at Grand Marais, Minnesota. The only restriction was no student instruction.

It appeared Dad's dream of flying hunters, campers, and fishermen into the wilderness areas further north was really taking shape.

In the meantime, the Krotz family had been growing, too. Mom (Dorothy Rindahl) and Dad married in 1946, Ginger was born in 1947, followed by me in 1948, and Clarice in 1949.

What was not taking shape, however, was the original Grand Marais airport, begun in 1933. I recall that Dad had been very skeptical about the town's airport layout, and his doubts proved correct. After 15 years of work, due to improper construction, the site failed to meet acceptable federal/state standards. It was granted only a limited license, which approved the field for flying for those who held a private license or better. It was noted that all pilots must be informed that the airstrip was 57 feet higher at the west end than the east end, with a grade of about 2.5 percent.

We girls were far too young to notice much of the grown-up goings-on for some time, but as we got older we became more involved in Mom and Dad's discussions. When we learned that Skyport airport was licensed ahead of the unfinished Grand Marais site, we assumed there must have been considerable frustration of some local officials, perhaps even embarrassment or resentment over the decision favoring Skyport airfield.

According to our parents, almost immediately after Skyport airfield was completed and licensed, the state informed Dad that his airport, if he wanted to keep it, could only be used as a private airport. If any commercial use was noted, the airport would be subject to confiscation. Private airports did not then, and I believe do not now, require state licensing. We still wonder if this demand was perhaps a politically coordinated "push back" to obtain our dad's finished airport.

Dad's response was one we'll always remember. He said, "I fought for freedom in the war, and now I have to do it all over again here. I simply don't know what to do now." This was a terrible blow to him after all the work he and Mom had invested in the place.

Dad was offered a $10,000 buy-out payment by the State of Minnesota for all his property, including the finished airport, except a small strip along the shore of Devil Track Lake where he ultimately built our home, a lodge, three cabins, and a campground. If he didn't accept this offer, the alternative was condemnation and seizure of the property by the state and get nothing.

Rather than lose it all, Dad opted to take the buy-out. The state then took ownership of the airport in late 1948. Dad would go on to manage the airport as a volunteer for the next 32 years. He was paid no salary for management or maintenance, but was allowed to sell aviation fuel and operate Skyport Lodge and his flying business.

On November 11, 1948, Skyport Lodge airfield was officially approved as the new Grand Marais airport. This decision resulted from a joint meeting between state, federal, county, and village officials as all other proposed sites fell short of official approval.

Despite this new strength, another influence was taking shape that would change the Arrowhead in the future. Not foreseen was growing state and national public opinion that growing airplane activity in the wilderness sections of St. Louis, Lake, and Cook Counties was increasingly a threat to wilderness solitude and the preservation of the lakes, streams, and forests in a natural condition.

In 1949, after considerable national public debate, President Harry S. Truman signed an executive order banning aircraft travel in these areas. This ruling banned flights over the restricted areas of the Superior National Forest after January 1, 1951, except where private holdings were currently served by plane. Those routes would be held open until January 1, 1952.

Finding financing to cover all the expenses associated with Skyport airfield, the lodge, and campground was no small task. It all added to the burdens Mom and Dad faced daily. As we realized over time, each of the financial demands required resolution, possibly more debt, and sacrifices for all of us. Each new loan meant our family had less money left over to buy the things we wanted. Thus, we all shared in the financial difficulties of living here.

Even with all this, our father was a very generous and compassionate man. We sisters only learned much later that he gave free flying lessons to several young men who could not afford to pay, even though our family certainly could have used the money. Our family never suffered because of his generosity, and these were worthy and much appreciated acts of kindness that influenced the lives of several young men in the community.

The poet, Virgil, said, "Fortune favors the bold." I am still so impressed that Dad was bold enough to pursue his dreams. He was young, highly focused, and talented in so many ways.

One thing is certain, establishing a wilderness-based airport opened the door to air travel into the Arrowhead region, and this growth in aviation would contribute to our family's survival.

Now all we needed was a plane of our own and Dad's dreams could really take flight.

CHAPTER 3:

Getting Our Wings

The J-3 Piper Cub after Kathy and Rodney Roy restored it.
PHOTO BY R. STRUCK

Early J-3s powered by 37-40-hp Continental A-40 engines.
Most J-3s powered by 65-hp Continental A-65 engines.

—*Piper's Golden Age,* by Alan Abel,
Drina Welch Abel, Paul Matt

KROTZ FAMILY 1941 J-3 PIPER CUB

Length: 22 feet, 4.5 inches
Height: 6 feet, 8 inches
Wingspan: 35 feet, 2.5 inches
Gross Weight: 1,220 pounds
Rate of Climb: 450 feet per minute
Operational Ceiling: 12,000 feet
Top Speed: 73 mph (one pilot and one passenger)

Landing Speed: 38 mph
Cruising Range: 220 miles
Fuel Capacity: 12 gallons
Fuel Consumption: 4.46 gallons per hour
Propeller: 72 inches Sensenich wood
Cost at Production: $1,395.00

Kathy standing next to the J-3 Piper Cub on skis.

As noted in the book, *Piper's Golden Age* by Alan Abel, Drina Welch Abel and Paul Matt, early J-3s were powered by 37 to 40-hp Continental A-40 engines. The majority of the J-3s, however, were built with a 65-hp Continental A-65 engine.

My 1941 J-3 has a length of 22 feet, 4 and a half inches; a height of 6 feet, 8 inches; a wingspan of 35 feet, 2 and a half inches; and a gross weight of 1,220 pounds. With a rate of climb of 450 feet per minute, an operational ceiling of 12,000 feet, and a top speed of 83 mph, it offers a cruising speed of 73 mph for one pilot and one passenger.

As a light airplane easy to handle, the J-3 has a landing speed of 38 mph, a cruising range of 220 miles, fuel capacity of 12 gallons, oil capacity of one gallon, and fuel consumption of 4.46 gallons per hour.

It features a 72-inch Sensenich wood propeller. At the time of its production, the price for a new J-3 was $1,395.

One truly good thing that really stands out was the arrival of a J-3 Piper Cub that Dad purchased in 1950. I was very young at the time, but I remember him telling Mom in a very excited voice how fortunate this was and how lucky they were to have found the Cub.

Introduced by the Piper Aircraft Corporation in 1937, the J-3 Cub quickly became a household name for a growing population of pilots in the U.S. In a few short years, the graceful yellow Cub would become an icon of America's fascination with flying, its appeal capturing my dad's interests as well.

We don't know exactly why Dad preferred the Cub, but it was already a national icon of flying and very popular with a variety of pilots. The Cub was an ideal bush plane that excelled in its ability to get into and out of small lakes and dirt strips, and was easy to maintain. You might say its reputation preceded itself.

Being in a large commercial aircraft today is quite different than flying the Cub. As a passenger in a modern jet passenger airplane, you are in a virtual cocoon, an artificial space devoid of the feelings of air currents, sounds, sights, and smells associated with small aircraft. Here, the value lies in a speedy arrival at one's destination, no matter the distance involved. Yet to me the joy of flight is missing. There is not much to do but to either read a book, sleep, or watch the plane's TV programs. You're simply on a winged bus.

I believe appearances matter. Likewise, love should be noticeable. Compared to the large old Ford Tri-Motor airplane that, in the early days, landed with skis on the Grand Marais harbor ice and later came to Skyport airport, the Cub was quite opposite in beauty. Where the silver-colored Ford aircraft was built with heavy corrugated metal sides and wings, few smooth surfaces, and three large exposed radial engines, the Cub was stunning with its delicate lines, small motor, vivid yellow color, and appearance of adventure. The graceful lines of the Cub compared to the Ford's metal box look clearly showed a difference in structure. The venerable Ford Tri-Motor simply does not have a handsome appearance. In fairness, of course, the large old Ford Tri-Motor was a major leap forward in carrying capacity and reliability of transportation. To be fair, a more apt comparison is that both aircraft were slow and reliable and did their jobs respectably.

With tandem seating and dual controls, the Cub was a natural fit for flight instruction, carrying one passenger, and with floats, getting into and out of remote lakes and waterways in the northern forest-lake region of the Arrowhead. There didn't seem to be anything the Cub couldn't accomplish, and it became a mainstay of transportation for guests at the lodge, fishermen heading north into remote lakes, corporate guests wanting to reach distant lodges throughout the region where float planes were allowed, and for delivery of supplies or other items needed in a hurry.

Since its introduction in 1937, the J-3 Cub's service history includes private flying, flight instruction, military service, search and rescue operations, Civil Air Patrol programs, construction duties, pipeline surveys, wildfire control, law enforcement, and many other activities keeping this icon of history alive and well.

Whether simple excursions over the regional forests nearby, a type of flying now called "flight-seeing," short destinations to deliver or pick up some item or person, instructing new student pilots, or trying out new techniques with floats on Devil Track Lake, the Cub performed handsomely.

Instruments were basic but are still used in much improved units in modern aircraft: tachometer, carburetor heat, oil temperature, oil pressure, altimeter, fuel primer, compass, and air speed indicator.

With an air frame of light tubing covered with high-strength cloth, many internal wires, cables and pulleys, gauges, glass, and a motor, to name a few components, the Cub was fairly easy to move by hand when on wheels.

Also, even though stored with floats in our lakeside hanger, it was not much physical effort to open the hangar door and pull the Cub out to the ramp. The Cub would be put into the hangar tail first so we could pull it out by the pontoons and down the ramp into the water, a short distance of about 20 feet. I always had someone hold one of our tie-down ropes to keep the Cub from going too far into the lake. Once secured to the dock, we would begin to load it. Then, when all was secure and we were ready to go, we'd start the engine. The Cub always stayed secured to the dock the entire summer.

The Piper Cub, in various models over the years, just doesn't fade away. Not only are many original Cubs restored and kept in prime operating condition by proud owners wanting a valued part of American aviation history, but today you can find modern reproduction Cubs manufactured to introduce student pilots and others to flying history and the fun of flying.

One such manufacturer is the American Legend Aircraft Company (ALAC) in Sulphur Springs, Texas. As noted on their website:

"ALAC produces the AL-3 Legend Cub, a modernized version of the venerable Piper J-3 Cub, one of the greatest aircraft ever built. The firm was founded expressly to develop a light-sport certified version of the venerable Piper Cub airplane, a beloved aircraft so pure in design and so honest in handling that something had to be done to keep them flying. It must look and feel just like the Original. And it does.

"ALAC notes that the Cub is low and slow and this makes flying a Cub so serene. Its large wings give it handling qualities that can only be described as Cub-like. It excels at slow flight and it begs to remain airborne with the slightest of winds. Several model options offer various engine sizes, performance and airplane accessories."

L TO R: Kathy, sister Ginger, and sister Clarice being held by their mother, Dorothy Rindahl Krotz, circa 1953.

CHAPTER 4:

Childhood Adventures

As Skyport Lodge and the airport grew, so did our family. First came Ginger, born January 24, 1947; later that year a Seabee made the first commercial flight service from Grand Marais to Isle Royale, and construction was completed at Skyport. I was born June 10, 1948, just a few months before Skyport was made the official airstrip of the county. And Clarice arrived on December 17, 1949; the same year the ruling was passed to ban air travel over the wilderness—though that didn't go into effect for another year or two. I was perhaps closest to my older sister, Ginger. Mom called us her twins. Clarice was the "third musketeer."

We initially lived ten years in a small two-story log cabin on Maple Hill, which was roughly 20 feet long by 15 feet wide, without water or electricity. Dad would later build another home for us on Maple Hill, but I remember the first cabin best. It had only a main room downstairs with a closet, and a small bedroom upstairs where we girls slept in the same bed together. When electricity was put in, there was only one light upstairs and down. Yet we also continued to play and read by the amber light of a kerosene lamp.

Our home at Skyport Lodge was on an old Ojibway settlement on Devil Track Lake. We were told that Devil Track Lake gained its name from old Sam Zimmerman who lived nearby. He was missing one leg and used two crutches to walk, for which he had made two small snowshoes so he wouldn't sink into the snow. One day, after he walked across the lake in the winter, the local Indians saw the unusual pattern of his three snowshoes and called it "the devil track!"

While rebuilding the lodge and adding six new motel-style guest rooms, Dad found what appeared to be an Indian bear claw necklace. The claws were uncovered in about a foot of dirt, placed in a near perfect half-circle. No cord was evident. The claws were displayed in the lodge for many years.

Also found were arrowheads and a rock about 5 inches by 7 inches that was chipped on one side to make a sharp edge and a groove that was brown in color, perhaps where a rawhide strap held a handle on. Did this serve as an axe? Dad also found an actual gold nugget while he and Grandpa Harry were digging a well for the lodge. Digging the well quickly took on new meaning after that!

Devil Track Lake is a narrow, east-west body of water of 1,838 acres, with a maximum depth of 50 feet of brown water. The lake is highly popular for fishing during open water for walleye, northern pike, smallmouth bass, lake whitefish, white sucker, and yellow perch. Ice fishing here is also popular. A U.S. Forest Service campground is located on the west end of the lake.

Although we were typical kids who would rather play than work, we all pitched in to help at an early age. We only did what small kids could do, but when our work was given our folks' approval, we rushed to find adventure outdoors and explore our natural surroundings, no matter the time of year or the weather.

Mom also was an accomplished seamstress who made most of our clothes, even our prom dresses. For our summer sun dresses, she would obtain used flour sacks and these became attractive dresses for each of us. Her musical talents were especially welcome during the cold winter months. She was a gifted self-taught player of the piano, mouth organ, accordion, violin, and pump organ. She was also active in the Ladies Aid Society of Bethlehem Church in town. She even became quite popular with the women on Maple Hill as she was self-trained in setting women's hair, setting perms, and styling it as they wanted.

On top of all this, Mom had artistic skills. We still have a treasured picture she drew and colored with watercolors of three little girls playing on the shore of Devil Track Lake. She captured each child's looks beautifully, and the picture always brings back fond memories of life at the lodge. She painted this picture long before we were born; was she anticipating three little girls of her own on a lake? I believe she was only 15 years old at the time.

Winter time was a particular challenge we enjoyed. Our folks closed the lodge and airport from October 15 to May 15. During this time Dad would travel to Chicago to work, so Mom was alone most of the time with three little girls in tow. Dad usually drove to Chicago, but in later years he would fly the Piper J-3 Cub and give flight instruction to earn extra money. He was the only flight instructor to give lessons there in a tail-dragger-type airplane. Dad's absence was felt by all of us, but Mom's relatives from the Rindahl family—long-time residents of the Maple Hill community who had emigrated in 1886 from Rindal, Norway—were available to help and keep tabs on us.

Playing in the snow alone, or with cousins or friends, was always a lot of fun, and we took advantage of it each day. When the snow plow came through on the dirt road next to our place, Ginger and I would climb on top of the high berm created by the large v-shaped plow, and walk on the crest of the ridge. If enough snow had been piled up, we would also dig into the base and make a tunnel in as far as we could. One of us would watch out for the plow so we could escape from our tunnels and climb up to safety on the top of the ridge until it had passed. Then we'd jump down and return to our tunnel. If we tired of this adventure, we'd often make an igloo closer to home.

There was also Pat's Pond up the road from us that the Iverson boys kept shoveled, so we spent a lot of time skating there and playing broom ball. And many a winter weekend was spent sliding and skiing on the hill in front of our house. Our cousins and friends would build a ski jump and maintain it all winter. We loved the Norwegian skis our Grandpa Henry Rindahl made for his seven children, which were passed on to us kids. I still own one pair of these wonderful skis. We would ski and slide until we got cold and tired, and then we'd go in and huddle around the wood stove while Mom made us some hot chocolate and popcorn. She would also offer cookies and dessert she might have left from the week.

Mom would also give us some old Sears or Montgomery Wards catalogs to look at in the evening on the living room floor. Catalogs in those days were filled with colorful illustrations and modern products beyond our wildest imaginations! We cut out pictures of clothing models to make paper dolls and kept certain items in our minds to think about, particularly when we went to bed at night. In the soft amber glow of an antique kerosene lantern—a cherished 100-plus-year-old gift from our grandparents—these catalogs opened up an entirely new horizon for young girls, and we were smitten by the fancy descriptive pages. We also did a lot of drawing, and Mom patiently hung up our artwork for all to see and admire, and especially so Dad could see them when he returned in the early spring.

As snow gradually melted in the spring, we often got stuck in deep, wet snow and couldn't move. The more we laughed and struggled, the more we got stuck! Then Mom would have to come out to rescue us, often with our feet coming out of our snow-filled boots when she pulled us free. It was all good fun in spite of us getting cold and very wet. I think Mom enjoyed it as much as we did.

One early spring, the river was high with rushing water. Ginger, Clarice, and I decided to visit our aunt's place to see a horse she had. We were in our early teens. To get to her place we either had to wade across the Devil Track River or walk the long way around on the nearby road. Mom advised us strongly to stay safe and take the road. Instead, and with an eye to more adventure, we chose to cross the river at a shallow place. The water was higher than expected with a strong current, but we went into it without hesitation.

Midway across the river, Clarice, who was wearing only moccasins on her feet, lost her footing. In the struggle to regain her footing, she lost one of the moccasins, and her jacket slipped off into the current. This was no ordinary jacket but Dad's actual flight jacket from the war, with all of his missions stamped on it and the U.S. Army Air Corps insignia! We desperately tried to catch the jacket but it was swiftly carried downstream, much to our horror. Now we had to return home and confess what happened.

Fearing the worst, we confessed to Mom and Dad and waited for the storm to begin. To our surprise, Dad looked at us carefully and then said, "Okay, then. You've disobeyed us, but I feel you've suffered enough by losing something of value of mine. Now, next time listen and obey our rules. Go outside and play." We never heard any more of this from either of them. This experience made us respect them all the more.

This wasn't the only time Dad showed his ability to make the best of things in a way that impressed us girls. His first airplane was a J-2 Piper Cub. Unfortunately, on a day of strong winds, Dad landed on our unfinished dirt strip without knowing that Grandpa Harry had

CHAPTER 4: CHILDHOOD ADVENTURES | 25

L TO R: **Clarice, Ginger and Kathy** in front of a log cabin, which was their first home on Maple Hill before the new house was built. The family had to have a home on Maple Hill because the road was not plowed all the way to Skyport in the winter. This dovetail log home was originally built by Mr. Skoglund in the late 1800s and was taken apart and moved by several families for a first home while they built a more permanent structure.

not cleared the larger rocks off the strip, as Dad had asked him to do; without a radio in the plane, he couldn't be alerted to anything of concern at home, so he brought the J-2 in. The Cub's propeller hit a large rock ruining the blade and engine. Dad knew right away that the Cub was damaged beyond repair. To lose a plane is a major loss, but at least he was not injured.

Dad removed the wings, and the body of the plane was placed behind the lodge where it became our new playhouse. Two of us would climb in and pretend to be flying, while the remaining sister would lift the plane tail up and make the plane move as in flight while imitating engine noise. We took turns and it was always great fun 'flying' our plane. Although an innocent playtime activity, it shows how much of our lives began to be centered on airplanes and flying.

Other fun times were had building tree forts and teepees in the woods near our house on Maple Hill. My sisters; our cousin Gary Rhindahl; and friends (all of Native American ancestry), Victor One Feather and Geraldine Tica Pederson; and Michael, Peter, and Bobby LeSage joined in. We used small poles and covered them with ferns. Moss was laid on the floor for comfort. Much time was spent renewing the fern covering as drying caused shrinkage and holes in the covering. By the end of the summer the teepee would have a very thick cover, but after the winter snow, it would be necessary to do it all over again in the spring.

And, of course, as soon as the Devil Track Lake water close to shore was warm enough, we spent as much time as we could swimming. We simply couldn't ignore the temptation of such a beautiful lake at our doorstep.

In the fall, Dad hosted Halloween parties for all three of our grade school classes. Our Uncle Jimmy would be in a back closet with a microphone connected to a pumpkin to make it "speak." Under dim light, Dad would tell spooky stories while passing around a bowl of oiled spaghetti and grapes (brains and eyeballs), and the skinned hands and feet from a bear that resembled the hands of a human. One girl got so scared she fell off the stairs she was sitting on!

Later on in high school, Dad sponsored a couple of dances, complete with music.

We were a tight-knit community up in the remote north, perhaps as in many small towns. We played together and grew up together, boys and girls alike, with no problems. That is, until we got somewhat older and some of the area boys wanted us to play football with them. Well, after a few short scrimmages we quickly learned that their combined weight and strength was too much for us, and we made some good excuses to not play. We had to rest and let our bodies and egos heal. This was the only concession we made to boys.

We all had school friends and cousins, and boys did interest us, but our folks needed our help around the airport and lodge, and actual boyfriends would have to wait for a while. This became an accepted lifestyle for all of us.

CHAPTER 5:

The Family Business

Running a lodge is truly a team effort every day of the year. From the beginning, Dad's mother, Dorothy, and her second husband, Harry Hadaway, who lived in Chicago, came up to be with us to help in the summer months. They did this for many years until she died in 1963. Then, Harry pulled a travel trailer up to the lodge and Dad hooked it up with water and electricity. Grandpa became our handyman of sorts and we loved having him with us.

Dad would also hire on some local men to continue to work on the airstrip, lodge, and out buildings. Good friends Bill and Jean Riley also helped, especially Bill, when he was a teenager. Jean was a great cook and often cooked for us when we had large numbers of guests present.

Since we girls were very young, we had heard Mom and Dad discuss aviation and its key role in making Skyport Lodge a reality; we learned a lot by listening. Incoming pilots and their families were our bread and butter, and our folks increasingly depended on us to help keep the lodge facilities clean and presentable, and to welcome both drive-in and fly-in guests.

With each passing year we girls got stronger, and our work expanded. We learned how to do laundry in an old wringer washer, how to hang clothes properly for easier ironing, and to fold clothes properly. We were glad when a laundromat opened in town. We started very young on the easy items: handkerchiefs, pillow cases, and sheets. As teenagers, we had to clean each of the three cabins and six motel rooms daily, as well as clear the tables in the lodge, clean the dining room, and wash the dishes… and go back outside to help the guests if necessary. We always did this work in our shorts or swim suits and summer tops and nobody seemed to mind, as living up north was always an informal lifestyle.

Skyport with the motel added on, circa 1960s.

Every Saturday morning at the lodge we worked on baking bread, cake, cookies, and other pastries for the rest of the week. Sunday afternoons, lefse was made from the leftover mashed potatoes from the chicken dinner we had after church. My mother used this opportunity to teach us these skills. We girls alternated baking a different treat each week, so we learned how to bake everything at a very young age.

We had plenty of work to do outdoors, too, like bailing water out of our rental boats and mowing the extensive grass areas around the lodge, the plane parking area, and along the airport runway. To do the mowing, Dad would hitch the sickle-bar cutter to the power wagon and I would sit on the seat of the cutter while he slowly moved forward. My job was to physically lift the heavy cutter bar by pushing on a metal pedal and at the same time, lifting a hand bar that lifted the fast moving blades to keep them from hitting rocks. Ginger did this chore more often than I did. Dad did eventually buy a gas push mower.

Gardening also came into play once the soil was warm enough, usually around the first of June. We judged this by putting our fingers in the soil and, if our fingers were still comfortably warm, we knew it was time to plant seeds. Our family garden was large. It measured about 50 feet wide by 100 feet long, and we packed as much in it as we could. Dad also built a greenhouse that produced many vegetables.

Our garden produced potatoes, lots of green beans, beets, peas, carrots, onions, rutabagas, cabbage, pumpkins, squash, and even some corn. We canned whatever we could, but the root vegetables could be kept stored well into the winter in a cool cellar room. I remember when Fisherman's Picnic was in town, Mom would make us cut up the green beans before she let us walk into town (about 5 miles) and enjoy the many festivities going on. Preparing and storing food was a way of life, and we learned much each year.

We weren't vegetarians. We ate lots of venison, even beaver. Mom's favorite meat was partridge. Once when driving on Devil Track Road, a partridge flew up and was hit by a car in front of us. The other car kept going, but not Mom. She got out to get the dead partridge. While she was doing this, another partridge flew into our car window. Mom got this bird, wrung its neck, and brought both birds home to clean for supper that night.

Speaking of birds, we had at least 25 chickens that Mom and Dad would butcher in the fall. Mom would can most of them for the winter. We also had lots of rabbits, anywhere from 50 to 100 at a time after they had babies. Then, there was always a dog and cats as our pets. At one time, Dad even had a Belgian horse.

We were very active in 4-H and worked very hard to win a first prize in each county fair entry, whether we showed a rabbit, chicken, or vegetable. We especially wanted a first prize as it came with $3 so we could buy some new school clothes. Because we were about the same size growing up, we could exchange clothes often. Ginger even won a trip to the State Fair in Minneapolis one year based on her winning dress design. She participated in a fashion show at Dayton's Department store that summer.

Even though we weren't farming, one hot summer day we cut about 40 bales of hay for our animals. We had a load of bales on the pickup truck, as well as on the trailer behind us. We were ecstatic about how much we had gotten done that day. We were dripping with sweat, hair amiss with hay sticking to our hair and clothes, but we didn't care how we looked, we were just pleased with our results. Dad was pleased, too. He said, "You're better than any boys!" We thought so, too.

Clarice, not so enthusiastic said, "I fail to see the fun in it." She then repeated herself loudly, "I fail to see the fun in it!" At this we laughed as we knew she was very academic, an honor-roll student and always studying—more than I can say for Ginger or myself. We always ragged her for finding ways to get out of hard labor, but we had to give her credit for always chipping in even if it was begrudging on her part. Tough physical work just wasn't her thing.

I remember one time when Mom sent us to the wood shed to fire up the wood stove for supper. I picked up a good armful of wood while Clarice just stood there making jokes. The more she joked, the more we laughed, and the more I dropped the wood. I finally had to use a stern voice to get her to help after she quipped, "That's the way the mop flops!"

Yet, we did a lot together and got along very well. Dad always said, "If you can't get along with each other, who can you?" We took this to heart and over the years, we three sisters were the best of friends.

If we weren't working or playing, school work filled our evenings. Because we didn't have a car, we couldn't participate in after school activities as we would not have a way to get home afterwards. I did work briefly at Leng's Soda Fountain in town, but I was bored and missed the challenging atmosphere and excitement of our lodge business. The dynamics of this environment are very vivid and I recall with satisfaction the times spent helping in so many ways.

As I look back, I realize we weren't really that much different from the other families living around us in the woods. In such a small community like ours, everyone worked together all the time; you were involved in your family's business whether it was farming, store sales in the village, education, logging and lumbering, commercial fishing, or, in our case, flying. All our friends were similarly occupied growing up. Now that I think about it, they didn't find our aviation business unusual. It was simply a way of life for the Krotz family.

CHAPTER 6:

A Family of Fliers

Fly-in guests were considered special, and we went out of our way to welcome them, provide fuel for their planes, and get them into the lodge for a warm meal and/or rooms. It was in this environment that the discussion of aviation, aircraft, and flying became quite natural for all of us, and we listened intently to our guests' stories and exploits.

Not knowing who would fly in or drive in made our contacts with these strangers both challenging and often rewarding. A lot of very important people came to our airstrip and lodge, and after we got to know each other they all seemed like an extended family. We even exchanged letters and holiday greeting cards, especially with repeat guests. One of our most frequent guests was Sherman P. Booen, former owner and publisher of *Midwest Flyer* magazine, who would arrive in his attractive Bonanza airplane.

If the pilots and passengers were hungry, we had them come to the lodge where we'd fry them a hamburger. Bill Bally, well-known local welder and machine shop operator in town, once asked us to prepare a hamburger with everything on it. Well, that's just what we did! Beginning with our homemade buns, we added a quarter-pound of fried hamburger, lettuce, onions, tomato, bacon, and mayo. Bill loudly proclaimed this "The Sky Burger" and it quickly became one of the most popular items on our menu.

As you might expect, our lodge became a meeting place to gather. It was open to anyone or any group, especially if it involved children. Kids were always my primary focus around the lodge and each new family brought us many new playmates over the years.

I vividly recall one family in particular. The couple had three young boys, ages 11 to 14, and there were three of us young girls of similar age hanging around. We got along very well and, while the adults chatted in the lodge dining room or around the fireplace, we'd go into an adjoining room and play table tennis, go outside to play, or just sit and talk down by the lake.

This family had another key ingredient that Dad relished. The man was a former German Luftwaffe pilot from WWII. After the war, he had emigrated to Argentina and then came to the U.S. and became an American citizen. He and Dad talked long into the evening, discussing their wartime exploits, each trying to outdo the other in relating their piloting records. When the evening got late, we'd often hear them stating proudly that their air force and planes were better than the other's. To this Dad would say in a loud voice, "Yes, but who won the war!" We often laughed when we heard this, Mom, too.

In the 1950s, the Cole Brothers Airshow out of Illinois spent time on the North Shore with their friends, the Dwight Keller family, who owned a resort on Pike Lake just west of us. Having arrived by air, the Cole Brothers put on a couple of airshows at Skyport airport, which most of the county residents attended. This was good for our business.

We would remove the front windows of the lodge and sell hot dogs, pop, candy, and other treats. At the end of a busy day, our family relaxed in front of the lodge, catching our second wind before beginning the clean-up, and then replacing the windows before mosquitos arrived in the evening. Our step-grandfather, Harry Hadaway, made a comment about having sold everything, including the hot dog he had kicked under the counter three times! We certainly laughed at this and always enjoyed his humor.

One of the most exciting times with aircraft came in 1962 when two large Ford Tri-Motor planes and two U.S. Forest Service water bombers landed one late afternoon to refuel, and for the men to rest prior to taking off the next morning to spray the area forests for army worm infestation. This small armada created a sound unlike anything else in the sky and we could hear them coming our way from a long distance. They were at Skyport airfield for at least a week, spraying before dawn every morning. The pilots were working for the State Forestry Department. We had to get up at 3:00 a.m. to prepare breakfast for them by 4:00 a.m. Their early flights were necessary before the winds came up.

When it came time to take off the next day, we watched with great anticipation as the Torpedo Bomber modified craft roared aloft with bright blue flames coming out the rear of its engine exhausts. The Ford

Tri-Motor craft were slower and appeared to just lumber down the runway until they had enough speed to lift off. They reminded us of large flying corrugated metal boxes, but we envied the pilots' abilities in operating such large planes.

Over the years, this northern base attracted many types of single and multi-engine aircraft, including Cessna, Piper, Mooney, Beechcraft, Taylorcraft, Stinsons, including the large Beavers made in Canada, DC-3s, and the distinctive Ford Tri-Motor transport. As plane technology advanced, private jet aircraft and even helicopters would fly in, along with the large twin-engine water bombers used by the U.S. Forest Service to fight forest fires.

As the years progressed, Dad's aviation dreams continued to unfold. He once commented that during the war he had never thought he'd see the lodge and all that we had accomplished so far, but his active regional promotion of the new Skyport airstrip was taking hold, and an increasing number of planes, equipped with floats, landed on Devil Track Lake. We also saw an increase in wheeled planes landing on the airstrip, and this really kept us busy.

We would rush to greet each plane and its passengers, clean their windshields, and fill the fuel tanks. Our fuel pumps were above ground and not electrically powered. So as a young girl, I had to literally hang on the long pump handle to pull it down to move fuel into the hose and into the plane. Our red pump held 80 octane fuel and the blue pump held 100 octane fuel. The pilots always seemed to trust us, and we did our best to do this correctly without spilling. Later, we had electric pumps and had 100 octane low lead fuel that could be used for all planes except jets.

My sisters and I started learning to drive when we were very young, a skill that would later prove very useful, and an adventure we all enjoyed. When Dad wanted to drive into town for something, he would have us sit on his lap and let us steer. Dad wanted to see how we reacted, and teach us how to watch for what was on the road ahead.

We'd often visit Grandpa Rindahl at his tiny watch repair shop. The small shop was a popular meeting place for the old men who filled

Clarence Krotz with the J-3 Piper Cub on floats, circa 1960s.

the space with their cigarette, cigar, and pipe smoke as they drank coffee and shared the latest gossip. We were always amazed at listening to the languages spoken, which included Norwegian, Swedish, German, and Ojibwemowin, to name a few. We stayed out of reach of the snuff chewers who used the spittoon frequently—with infrequent accuracy.

At the ripe age of 13, Dad started to teach me to drive an old 1950s era Ford sedan. It was stick-shift style, quite a challenge to learn at first, especially to coordinate a clutch pedal and the gas pedal. I also learned to drive an old olive army panel truck, called a Dodge power wagon. Because the heavy-duty truck had four-wheel drive, it did a lot of hard work around our place, especially to grade the original airstrip as it was being built. (It was this truck that Dad drove to Duluth to get me and Mom after I was born, a round trip of over 200 miles. The old military truck had no amenities and I'm sure Mom was very uncomfortable both going to Duluth and on the way back home.)

As active teenagers, we loved to drive any of the family vehicles whenever we could. Our folks didn't mind as long as we stayed on our property and drove safely. One of the best times was when incoming pilots would call ahead at night to alert us to their arrival. In the early years, our airstrip didn't have adequate night lighting, so when Dad received a pilot's request to light the runway, we were called into action, no matter the time of night.

Ginger would drive one vehicle and I would drive another. We'd quickly make a pass down the length of the runway to scare the deer off, then one of us would park facing across the runway at one end, and the other facing down the runway from the other end. This was a big help to the pilots, and we enjoyed our part in making their arrivals safe. We were about 12 or 13 years old at the time and thought it was great fun.

Dad also frequently drove guests into the village for shopping, then returned later to pick them up to come back either to the lodge or to depart in their planes. Once we girls had our driver's licenses, this became our job as well.

Compared to today's public FBOs (Fixed Base Operators), our operation was strictly a family affair. Our customers were a melting pot of life and we never knew who was coming to either visit briefly or stay for a few days. We greeted them all warmly and appreciated their financial support and compliments as well. And, sometimes, one of our guests would write to announce that they had decided to get into flying. This really pleased us.

CHAPTER 7:

Flight Notes

"Ask the pilots, and they'll confess that flying is more than just a means of getting around. It's about meeting the challenges of climate and terrain. It's about the extraordinary landscape beneath their wings. And foremost it's about the aircraft—the intense relationship and long-standing loyalty between pilots and their planes."

Alaska's Bush Planes by Ned Rozell

Once the summer months passed, we knew it would soon be time to store the Cub for the coming winter. To do this, Dad had to remove the Cub's wings to fit the fuselage into the hangar at an angle. The hangar really only had room for one plane, and we also had to put in the Piper Tri-Pacer, acquired in 1959, when one of Dad's major corporate clients, John Ruan, asked him to pick out a plane that would carry four people comfortably. Mr. Ruan owned Ruan Transport Company and he had a lodge on Brule Lake for his family and business clients.

Dad chose the newly introduced Tri-Pacer, a three-wheel, tricycle landing gear plane with an attractive interior. Instead of wheels, however, this plane was outfitted with floats. The Tri-Pacer was faster, had a more powerful engine, and carried more weight than the Cub. When not using the Tri-Pacer for this client, Dad had permission to use it for personal use whenever he wanted, as long as he did the maintenance and kept it ready at all times.

So, the Cub's wings were stored alongside its body, to be reinstalled in the spring. We all helped hold up the wings while Dad disconnected them. Even when stored, to me there was a look of dignity and tradition with the Cub, and I felt sorry that it had to endure a cold winter all alone. In the spring we'd reverse the process. When all was reassembled, Dad would take the Cub up to put it through its paces to ensure it was safe to fly for the coming season.

My sisters didn't find maintenance and service tasks desirable, but to me they seemed natural and I truly enjoyed them. I guess it's the totality and satisfaction of the experience that defines what I enjoy about flight. Grease, fuel, or oil on my hands or clothes was all part of this connection.

Apart from winter, the Cub was always on floats. When I wanted to get the Cub up our ramp out of the water, I'd center the Cub's nose on the ramp, get real close, and then gun the engine. The Cub would easily move up the ramp on its floats to a point where I'd cut the power, turn off the motor, and securely tie the plane down. Going up or down the ramp was always easy in years past as we used old engine oil to liberally grease the float groove in the ramp, a practice not allowed today.

The Cub got a lot of use doing a little of everything. Dad used it for anything, from hauling materials to taking aerial photographs for friend and local real estate agent Van Johnson, and everything in between.

Where charter flights were permitted, he brought people into remote areas to fish or camp. To better serve clients who wanted to fish, Dad provided minnows harvested from traps from several local small lakes, or pot holes, as he called them. Monker Lake, about 4 miles south of us, was his preference not only for the abundance of minnows, but also because he could fly in and out comfortably in the Cub. Actually, this was no small task as a full minnow tank with water added many pounds of weight. To gain enough speed to take off, Dad had to make continuous circles in the lake to build up speed, even banking the Cub to allow only one float to skim the surface and then fly off.

One summer, Dad gave rides to tourists out of the Grand Marais harbor; he charged $2.50 per person for a 15-minute ride. On one such sightseeing trip, Dad first stopped at Leng's Fountain in town, bought a quart of ice cream, had it double wrapped in newspaper, and then flew to the lodge and dropped the ice cream to us! The surprise package landed in tall grass in good shape. It was ice cream by airmail ahead of its time, and I had it for my birthday with strawberry shortcake. What a treat!

An Unusual Passenger

One summer day, I was preparing to shove the Cub away from the bank where it was tied up. I had just untied the rope and was going to jump aboard when I heard Dad yell, "Look out for the bear cub!" Well, I looked back to the other float and there was a small black bear cub holding onto it. I shooed him off and he swam to shore and scrambled away. Bears are our neighbors, and I took this as a good omen for the flight ahead.

The Cub was also used to look for lost or stranded campers or hikers. One summer, Dad flew into a remote lake to bring back a dead body. I happened to be home when Dad returned with his special cargo. The deceased was in a full-length heavy-duty bag that was strapped to one of the Cub's float struts. I could see the strange package as he slowly taxied to our dock. I helped him tie up the Cub and watched while he and a friend removed the dead person and took him to a waiting vehicle. Although I'll never forget this experience, I'm sure Dad didn't think much about it.

I recall a scare in the early years when a really bad storm was coming from the west to our place fast. Dad was just returning from a business trip in the Cub and, when he landed, he yelled for us all to come out and help tie it down quickly. We also double-tied other planes parked there as best we could.

As we didn't have a hangar available, Dad double-tied everything tightly, then put me in the luggage space behind the rear seat of the Cub with Clarice in the rear seat. He sat up front to keep the engine running at full bore. Grandpa Hadaway stood on one of the floats and this gave added weight to help the four of us "ride" out the storm. This storm was so bad that it almost blew out all the large west windows of the lodge! Ginger, Mom, and some of our guests actually saved most of the windows by moving back and forth across them with their hands to reinforce the loose panes. We did have a lot of water and some broken glass in the lodge, but in spite of the storm, none of the planes were damaged.

When time allowed, and we were very young and small, Mom and us girls would pile into the Cub and Dad would take us up for a pleasure ride that could last 15 minutes or an hour, depending on our endurance while crammed into the small back seat space that was meant for one person. No matter how uncomfortable we were, we loved flying in the Cub. Our family excursions became much more comfortable in the Tri-Pacer, and though I later enjoyed flying co-pilot with Dad in the Tri-Pacer, it always felt more like driving in a car than flying.

As a certified flight instructor, Dad gave flying instructions, both in Chicago and on the North Shore. Though Mom truly enjoyed flying, she never cared to go for her pilot's license, but we girls were eager to learn how to fly.

CHAPTER 8:

Learning to Fly

Kathy's sister, Ginger, getting ready for her first solo flight. A crowd had gathered, including someone from the newspaper, to come and watch. She took off just fine, and when landing, she gave the Krotz whistle (a whistle that her father would give when he flew by someone) and landed perfectly around the point out of view of the crowd, just incase she had a bumpy landing she didn't want them to see.

As a girl I always felt it natural to learn to fly. I don't recall any hesitation or fears along the way, and each new flight added to my zest for this exciting experience. I don't recall anyone telling us they thought it strange that the young Krotz girls were flying a yellow plane around the area. Dad certainly showed no hesitation to encourage us, and I'm sure we would have tangled with anyone who really gave us a hard time.

It's a wonderful feeling to be able to fly a light, responsive plane such as the Cub. I was very easy on the controls, even with the constant noise and buffeting of the wind surrounding me. I only weighed about 110 pounds as a teen, compared to the Cub's 900 pounds, including floats, but I believe a girl's touch can make a difference in this situation. The Cub seemed to know how much I wanted to fly, and I had the weird feeling that my bond with the Cub would grow over time.

Showing what we could do was Dad's objective when teaching us the tricks of the trade. He wanted us to make good decisions and to take control of whatever situation came our way in flight. Perhaps what made my training flights so unique was that our Cub was on floats all summer and this meant all take-offs and landings were on Devil Track Lake. That wasn't the average experience for a new student pilot, and though I did get to ride along with other pilots in wheeled planes, I never flew one myself until I was older and taking paid instruction. Flying with floats was all I knew when I was young, and I loved it. Devil Track Lake, with its approximate 7-mile length, was an ideal place to learn.

I don't recall any other float planes using the lake as much as we did, except for Luigi (Warren) LaPlanta who lived just down the lake from us and owned a Seabee plane, a modern, all-aluminum craft with stylish rounded lines and the ability to land on water or a runway.

In September of 1947, the first commercial air service arrived in the Grand Marais harbor, a single-engine amphibious Seabee for flights along the North Shore and air transport to Isle Royale. The all-metal Seabee can land both on water and land, and had a reversible propeller to move it backwards from a dock or shoreline. Dad liked the Seabee and found it highly suitable for his needs, both with the lodge and for traveling inland to northern lakes.

There's a whole different feeling to landing and taking off on water, and Dad had me practice in the center of the lake. No matter how many times I've flown the Cub, every take-off and flight brings excitement and sheer pleasure to me. The Cub's high wing placement allows a pilot to watch the floats as they gently enter the water, while also keeping an eye on the shoreline. Getting too close to shore could mean hitting a partially submerged log or boulder. While landing on water is challenging, I prefer it as I can see the wake of the floats behind me. You have no tracking sign on pavement airstrips.

Landings are fun but occasionally I bounced the Cub because I landed too hard. Ouch! Dad always said that I should try to "grease" them in a perfectly smooth landing. I'd practice "touch and go" flying on calm water, but if the water surface was rough, then I'd try to just skim the surface first to get a feel for conditions.

Dad taught me that you should always land or take off into the wind, so I learned to be alert for shifting winds. Sometimes, the circumstances were such that I'd have to take off or land crosswind. I've never felt intimidated by crosswinds, but I've never tempted fate and flown in really adverse weather or high winds. As the saying goes, "There are old pilots and there are bold pilots. But there are no old, bold pilots." I know a lot of pilots are extremely bothered by tricky crosswinds but I always enjoyed the challenge and became quite proficient in crosswind landings in the Cub. So far, so good.

Dad also trained each of us in "dead stick" landing. He'd take the Cub up to a certain altitude and then announce "engine out" as he greatly reduced the power. Wow! Talk about excitement and intense concentration fueled by complete silence except the wind rushing by as you maneuver the plane for a smooth landing on the water, applying power just before touching the lake surface! Over time we became quite proficient in this procedure to Dad's satisfaction.

In most cases, I would fly at an altitude of 1,200 to 2,000 feet. It was easier to see things and when I wanted to practice putting the Cub through controlled stalls, I would need the higher altitude. I know a lot of pilots don't care for stalls, but I enjoyed them. A stall is simply pulling up the Cub's nose with no additional power added. This drains lift from the wings until the plane shudders and slips briefly backwards, tail first. Once you push the nose down and power is restored, you build up speed and, when enough wind is under the wings, the plane resumes normal flight. It's certainly not likely to happen every flight, but it's very useful to know how to control a plane if and when stalls occur.

One of Dad's other suggestions was to practice flying a zig-zag course above (between) a line of power poles. He also suggested I pick out something on the ground and then fly around it in a circle, holding my wing tip on a "fixed" spot, to build up my confidence in holding a tight flight pattern. These are good skills for any pilot to have, and they're fun, too.

This training is especially helpful when you participate in a ground search for a lost plane, hunter, hiker, or canoe camper, or to conduct a wildlife survey. It's not unusual for law enforcement or conservation authorities to occasionally call on private pilots to help in these circumstances, an appeal we'd gladly respond to whenever we could. With its wrap-around windows and half-door set-up, the Cub was ideally suited for air and ground observations.

This feature was also conducive to aerial photography, something the Minnesota Department of Natural Resources has employed for over 60 years on wildlife or forest surveys. With growing confidence in my piloting, Dad would occasionally take me with him in the Cub to photograph someone's lakeshore lodge or other property that was for sale. Dad would sit in the front seat with his trusty camera, and I'd fly the Cub wherever he instructed me so he could get the best angle. Flying slowly in repeated circles with less than 1,000 feet of altitude was really fun.

CHAPTER 9:

Rite of Passage

Our family didn't always have a car, but we always had a plane, and this set us apart from our friends. While most of my peers looked forward to getting their driver's licenses, I wanted my pilot's license more than anything. Ginger, Clarice, and I each eagerly anticipated a rite of passage unique to our family of fliers: our first solo flights on our 16th birthdays.

To finally fly solo (alone, without anyone else, including the instructor), the instructor had to feel you were ready, and you had to accumulate at least eight hours flight training. Most student pilots had at least ten hours, but this could vary depending on the student pilot's abilities and preparation. I probably had over eight or nine hours, thanks to Dad's confidence in my growing skills and the freedom he granted me to fly.

But as the long-anticipated summer of 1964 progressed, my flights were fewer. My 16th birthday came and went without a solo flight. Ginger had already soloed, and Dad was busy training Clarice, as well as some local boys. Fall comes early up north and signals the end of another season of flying for the J-3 Cub; as Dad was not here during the winter, I worried we would soon have to store the Cub until the next spring. Dad was a patient man and wouldn't approve a first solo flight unless he was confident the student was ready. It would be awfully hard to have to wait all winter long for my turn.

But on July 31st, after we had landed and taxied to our dock, Dad said, "Do you want to try it now?" My only thought was, "Oh good, finally!" My moment had come at last.

Though Dad preferred to sit in the front seat when flying alone, as he knew he could handle anything affecting the plane's performance, I flew from the rear seat. This was noted in the Cub's flying directives, and was required to keep the plane's weight balanced. This also gave me an advantage to see things better outside as the engine in flight would raise slightly and this would partially obscure the horizon in front of me.

Officially flying solo, with Dad observing me from the ground, meant I was too busy to look around. I had to concentrate on the plane and where I was. The time aloft rushed by, and too soon I had to return home. Honestly, it wasn't scary at all. It was a real relaxing time. To me it was and remains a form of meditation. The only thing that bothered me was the potential risk of wrecking the Cub with Dad watching. I knew I didn't want to land in front of our lodge; I just didn't want anyone to see in case I bounced the landing. So I landed, successfully, way beyond the nearest point and took my time returning to our dock. My folks were concerned when I didn't immediately appear, so a friend got into his boat and roared over the lake to find me. He was much relieved to discover me safe and slowly returning. My reward was warm praise from Mom and Dad. I had finally soloed!

Perhaps flying is no different from other human passions, but for me it became something I needed and wanted to do whenever I could. Dad realized my growing skills and often allowed me the privilege to fly alone around our home area. I would take the Cub up to explore the north country surrounding our lodge. I'd fly over Pike Lake, Two Island Lake, Fish Lake, and other small lakes to see who was fishing or boating. Folks would often hear me coming and would come out to the shoreline from their cabins to wave.

One of the great pleasures of flying the Cub has always been its slow pace, allowing me to scan not only the horizon, but also what's beneath my wings. The Superior National Forest is an almost unlimited tapestry of ever-changing green, brown, black, blue, and other hues all stitched together, bordered on one side by the vast and beautiful blue of Lake Superior. This array below changes with the seasons and never fails to delight the eye. I'm sure the birds of the air would attest to this, as would other pilots. This is the realm where the Cub is in its glory, and I was always delighted to witness the vivid natural displays surrounding me.

There were times, however, both then and now, when I felt the urge to do something different, to combine my flight with an exciting twist and to put the Cub into "attack" mode. Don't get me wrong, the Cub is a far cry from a fighter plane. Yet this never stopped me. I'd pick out a small island in one of our area lakes, put the Cub into a slight wing downbank, cut the power somewhat, and descend rapidly. At the right moment just before reaching the island, I'd apply power, lift the nose of the Cub and fly away, satisfied that I had "bombed" my target. Other times, I'd look for someone by their cabin or in a boat, put the Cub into a modest dive, focus on coming close and watch their faces as I flashed by. I did this once when one of my sisters and her boyfriend were sunning themselves on a dock at our lodge, and my close pass really startled them!

I always was the daredevil of us sisters, and one day, when we had a lot of friends over, I thought it would be fun to do something to get their attention. I took off from the water, made a few quick circuits around our area, then headed back home. I came in with a slow descent and just missed a power line near where people were gathered. This really scared Mom and she screamed. But I came in just over their heads and landed without incident. All Dad said was, "I think she needs more dual time."

On another occasion, I flew the Cub to the mouth of the Devil Track River on the shore of Lake Superior. I proceeded up the river as it wound up the hill to the north, the sides of the river getting closer by the minute. Just before I reached the end on higher ground, I lifted the Cub's nose and we flew away, unscathed.

Though I believed that Dad would understand my desire to sometimes push myself with deep dives and aggressive piloting, such as he had excelled at during the war, I never mentioned this particular flight to him. I suspected he wouldn't approve of such needless risks. But one day, he was with me as I was flying the Cub. (He was in the front seat but I was flying it from the rear, using the rear control stick, throttle, and rudder pedals.) Dad turned around and said, "I have the controls," then took over and flew us to Inga's small farm. Inga was a great-aunt who lived nearby in a two-story house with a small barn beside it. I had no idea what he was planning.

Dad brought the plane into a fast dive toward her place and just before reaching her buildings, he banked the Cub. With the wings almost in a vertical position, he flew us between Inga's buildings. Then he brought the Cub up, leveled the wings and headed to Devil Track River where he flew right down the river so low that I thought that surely this time the wings would scrape the rocks on each side.

Wow, talk about a rush! What a flight! Back on level flight he turned around and said, "I used to do that flying at 200 mph in the war."

My life was far removed from any wars, but nevertheless I wondered what flying adventures were in store for me. Would I have my own fast plane? Would I want to be a military or commercial pilot? Or would I be content with something like the J-3 Cub? Whatever the future held, it seemed clear that it was only a matter of time before I went for my private pilot's license, and for that I would have to officially solo under an instructor's watchful eye. That wouldn't happen for another decade, but sometimes you have to go where the wind takes you, as trusting of season and instinct as the wild birds of the air.

CHAPTER 10:

New Horizons

In 1966, I graduated from high school, and the following year I went to Minneapolis where Clarice was studying at the University of Minnesota. We'd always viewed her as the brainy one, but she was also a little on the wild side, so I kept an eye on her. We lived together in Minneapolis and I worked to help with her rent, food, and other expenses so she could focus on her schoolwork.

But every spring, when she was out of school, I would quit my job and come back and work at the lodge. Every fall we'd move back to the Twin Cities and I'd have to find a new job, but that didn't bother me—I wouldn't have missed a summer up north.

I suppose folks would guess that I'd return to Cook County full time after Clarice was done with her schooling, but I met Bob Sopoci at a party and, you could say, my flight "altered course."

Bob was a friend of our roommate, Betty, and we ended up seeing quite a bit of him. When I first encountered him he struck me as the loud and overbearing type, but he was very persistent—one of those "this is how it's gonna be" guys. Even his family was involved. When I was away, he'd have his brothers and sister call me saying, "Bob misses you. Bob can't take his tests at college: he needs you."

Ginger always said I was too easygoing with him, but one thing led to another, and in 1970 Bob and I married. On September 20, when I was 22 years old, my first child was born.

It was a beautiful day on Devil Track Lake, and I was perched on top of a plane putting in fuel when the labor pains started. I wasn't due for some time, so at first I was sure it was mushroom poisoning because I'd just eaten some pizza topped with wild mushrooms Dad had foraged near the airport grounds. But it wasn't long before I realized I needed to head into Grand Marais to the hospital. Later that day, Lieschen Gayle Sopoci, or, as Dad called her, "The Little Storm of Devil Track Lake," was born.

Now, I had no intentions of leaving Skyport after Lieschen was born, but Bob wanted me to move to Minneapolis where he was still in college at the University of Minnesota. So, his parents drove up to "help" me pack and persuade me to get in the car. My mother-in-law, Florence, held Lieschen in her arms the whole way down (this was in the days before car seats, of course). My daughter didn't sleep a wink—and I wondered if she sensed my dismay at us leaving the lodge.

That was the beginning of a long hiatus from not just pursuing my pilot's license but also flying at all. We quickly went from a family of three to a family of five. By 1973, we had three children under the age of 3 years old: our son, Laetham, and daughter Steina, were only ten months apart. I didn't have time or money for a coffee break, much less flying.

When Lieschen was going into kindergarten, Bob and I built a house in Brooklyn Park, not far from where his parents lived. Back then, it was a quaint suburb with bunny rabbits running through the backyard, potato farms, and plenty of woods for the kids to build forts. (Things have surely changed!)

During the winters in the Twin Cities, I'd occasionally take odd jobs. Over the holidays I worked nights as a gift wrapper for Dayton's Department Store. I also worked at a nursing home and a bank, and babysat neighbor kids. My children didn't like it when I had to work nights. They would all cry and watch out the window for me to come home. But now they say they can relate, as most parents can, to that delicate balance of dreams, family time, and making ends meet. But no matter the challenges of the year, there was the promise of summer at the lodge. In fact, in all the years my family owned Skyport I never missed a summer.

So began the Sopoci-Krotz yearly "Great Migration." Just like the birds, we migrated north in the summer and south in the winter. Every fall we would pack up and head back to the Twin Cities for Bob's teaching job in Minneapolis, and every spring we would drive up the North Shore so I could work at Skyport. Bob would spend his days working for the DNR and his evenings catching his limit of walleye on Devil Track Lake. The kids would spend summers swimming in the lake, fishing, catching crawfish and minnows, playing hide and seek in Dad's campground, and sunning themselves on the airstrip blacktop. Not a bad life.

Our neighbors in the Twin Cities would tell us how lucky we were to vacation every summer up north and I'd laugh. "Vacation! Huh, I work hard all summer long!"

By the time the kids woke up each summer morning, I was already at work. They'd make their way down the walk from our little cabin (no hot water, shower, or TV) to the main lodge. Lieschen still remembers how she could smell the coffee brewing and the bacon frying, and how the lake would glisten peacefully in the morning sun. But when she'd open the back door to the kitchen, serenity disappeared. There I was, running around like a chicken with its head cut off, filling guests' breakfast orders, answering the phone, and manning the cash register.

Mom worked hard in the kitchen, but she was very shy and didn't like to deal with the customers. Dad, of course, loved joking and making conversation with the guests—both tourists and folks from town would come and listen to his stories. We never hired help except for Jean Riley, our smorgasbord cook. That meant I was the head cook, baker, waitress, air traffic controller, cashier, hotel maid, laundry lady, airplane fueler, car rental agent, and the entire guest services department for Skyport—to name just a few roles.

I took reservations, and when guests arrived in the middle of the night, I was the one who got them settled in. Then, when they wanted to go to town, I arranged car rental, or boat rental for their excursions on the lake. I ran the air traffic controls and guided pilots in, and then tied down and fueled their planes. I cleaned cabins and hotel rooms, and washed the laundry. I baked all the bread for our famous Friday spaghetti dinners, waited tables, and then zipped into the kitchen and made food for the very guests I took the orders for.

I loved the hustle and bustle of lodge life, and it was a thrill to see the yellow Cub tied up at the dock. I really enjoyed giving plane rides, and the memories of my own rides when I was much younger came rushing back. Just knowing the Cub was there gave me a warm connection to all that our family experienced in the northwoods.

The one thing that was missing was that long held dream: getting my pilot's license and truly taking flight.

CHAPTER 11:

Long-Awaited Dreams

Kathy Krotz-Finn with the J-3 Piper Cub on skis. PHOTO BY R. STRUCK.

As the cliche goes, where there's a will there's a way, and Dad, who had a habit of finding the way, decided he was going to help me fulfill my dream of getting my private pilot's license. Fifteen years after my first solo flight, he offered to pay for lessons with an instructor in the Twin Cities, and I started taking night classes at the Crystal airport. It wasn't too far from our winter house, but at times it was tough at home because Bob wasn't very supportive of my flying. He seemed to resent having to take care of three kids one or two nights a week, while I was in flight school. I wasn't gone for more than a couple hours at a time, but to the kids it felt like days. They'd wait up for me to come home, or sit with me at the kitchen table and look over my shoulder as

I studied clouds and constellations from my text books. I taught them the difference between cumulonimbus clouds and stratus clouds, and how to find Orion's Belt and the Big Dipper.

"Flying with Mom"

"The only time I remember flying with my mom was once when I was pretty little, maybe first grade, and we were living in the Twin Cities. Mom rented a plane from the Crystal airport, and I was in the passenger seat up front next to her. I saw all of the controls in the cockpit and thought, 'how does she know what to do with all of this?' I remember how fast the takeoff felt, but mostly I remember how my mom turned into a different person when she was flying the plane. I thought she was a lunatic, flying in what I thought was an erratic manner, making one wing go vertical pointing up towards the clouds and one pointing down towards the city highway. We buzzed over Minneapolis and I could see Highway 694; the cars looked like tiny ants. I remember as the plane turned, I slid up against the window and looked down. I was so scared, too scared to even cry. To this day I don't like heights!

—**Lieschen (Sopoci) Schoenert** *(Kathy's daughter)*

One of my instructor's comments was, "The most important thing to know is to know your limitations." It sometimes seemed that the way I found my limitations was by pushing right up against them. Though I had lots of experience flying up north, I still had plenty to learn and practice. My training plane was now an all-metal Cessna 152, a two-seater where pilot and passenger sat alongside one another, in contrast to the tandem seating of the Cub. It was difficult at first to get used to it, and I missed the Cub. The Cub was always on floats, so I had to learn how to handle landing on wheels. (I managed it, but to this day I prefer floats in the summer and skis in winter.)

One training flight was particularly memorable. My instructor and I were on our final descent, or approach, to the Crystal airport when a close encounter really scared us. Just as we turned our base leg (a short approach perpendicular to the runway), a larger and very fast single-engine plane cut right in front of us, in spite of our approach having been approved by the tower controller. There was no warning from the tower that this plane was in our air space, or that it needed to come in first. I kept my head and we landed safely, but my instructor was just as jolted by this close call as I was.

Nonetheless, I kept flying, encountered no more such trouble, and the hours and lessons accumulated. Just like during the summer I turned 16, I could hardly stand the anticipation of my first official solo flight for another instructor. The long-awaited day came, and he suggested a trip distance of at least 300 miles, which would also fulfill my cross-county requirements; I chose a long loop to Grand Rapids and back.

My plane's compass didn't work that well, so I generally followed roads. But as I neared Grand Rapids, a thick bank of fog rolled in and totally covered the town. Now I really was nervous. I had to find the airport and land. I cautiously circled the area at a low altitude. I circled and circled. Where was I? How would I complete my flight? Then, forms emerged from the fog: the three tall smokestacks of the well-known paper plant.

What a relief—now I could orient myself. I quickly headed to the airport. It was very windy there, but I didn't have any trouble during my approach or in making a crosswind landing. I taxied to the fuel pump, topped off the tanks, signed the guest register, and took off for the return flight without any further challenges. I must admit, when my wheels touched safely down once more in Crystal, I couldn't wait to tell my fellow student pilots at the Flying Scotsmen flying club about my achievement.

Some achievements are great because they challenge your skill, others challenge fortitude, others patience, and on and on in every imaginable combination. I had waited a long time for this dream, and it had waited for me. I don't regret the many sacrifices made in order to raise a family. I think that's what any parent would do. It's certainly the example my parents set for me, and the example I hope I've set for my kids, too. Sometimes you have to put a dream on the back burner. Sometimes you have to navigate by feel; sometimes the signs aren't so obvious, and the fog is thick, but if you take your time and stick with it, I believe you will find your way.

Thanks to my parents' support and my instructor's thoughtful training, I preserved and officially earned my private pilot's license in

1979, at 31 years old.

Not long after, in 1980, another dream came true: the Sopoci-Krotz family migrated up north one last time and stayed permanently. It was an easy decision to make: Bob was laid off from his teaching position in Minneapolis, he loved to fish and hunt, and I loved Skyport. Mom and Dad gave us a plot of land on Maple Hill to build a house, and the kids were officially enrolled in Cook County schools. We were chasing that north wind.

CHAPTER 12:

Grounded

L to R: Gary Schlienz, Steina Sopoci, Clarice Krotz, Ginger Berglund, Alonzo Krotz (Clarence's older brother), Dorothy Rindahl Krotz, Bob Sopoci, Laetham Robert Sopoci, Lieschen (Schoenert) Sopoci, Gary Wade Schlienz, Edmund Krotz (cousin to Kathy), Kathy, and Aunt Sis (Clarence's Aunt). This picture was taken in the early 1980s shortly after Clarence Krotz passed away.

Because we were focused on our own lives and families, neither Ginger, Clarice, nor I paid much attention to Dad's health. Perhaps like many people, we just assumed that our parents were fine and doing well. However, Dad was a hard worker under growing stress. His active physical commitment over the years to aviation, the lodge, and our family took its toll on him, and he suffered three heart attacks. Dad had already realized he would no longer pass the medical exam to fly, and had disassembled the Cub, around 1970, to rebuild some parts. Not long after my family and I moved north, the day came when he knew he needed to step down from running the lodge. I would have loved to have taken it over, but Bob was not interested, so the lodge was sold.

In 1965, the state deeded the airport to Cook County. Shortly after this, the county paved the runway and obtained a UNICOM radio system. I was the first one to officially operate this system. Dad continued to manage and maintain the airport without compensation. Toward the end of his tenure here, the county paid a portion of his electric bill for the operation of the UNICOM system. We are not aware of any other compensation for Dad's contributions to the operations of the airport.

Instead, I took a hard labor job at Hedstrom's Lumber Company. I'm what you might call petite, but I was piling lumber and bagging woodchips all day. It was tough work, and the aches and pains meant I always smelled like freshly sawed trees—and Bengay cream. The Cub didn't fly and neither did I, and I was certainly "knowing my limitations." But there were greater tragedies to come. On May 30, 1981, at 61 years young, and less than a year after selling Skyport Lodge, Dad suffered his final heart attack.

On the day he died he was stocking the pond and giving the pastor a tour of his garden. They were talking about death. My daughter, Lieschen, was there and remembers it still.

The pastor said, "Well, you're retired," as if that could convince Dad to take it easy. "I have too much to do!" Dad replied. He was always working on things for his grandchildren: he had a pony for the kids to ride, he was collecting wooden horses to build a carousel, and a lot more, and he listed them all off. Then, in the middle of this litany of labors of love, his heart gave out and he collapsed into the pastor's arms.

Dad was laid to rest in the Maple Hill Cemetery. In recognition of his substantial commitment to aviation, the Cook County commissioners voted to name Skyport airfield the Clarence Krotz Memorial Airfield. In August 1982, a special ceremony was held at the airport to unveil the new sign, and a reception followed at Skyport Lodge. His extensive military training and service, his discipline in managing the many and varied tasks of the airport, his awareness of the present and future value of aviation, his willingness to take risks, and his commitment to Cook County and its residents are the hallmarks of a true Renaissance man. I was proud that he was honored by our community.

But even more, I was, and am, grateful for his encouragement and guidance, for his extensive flying background, and for the many, many memories of flights together. We talked about so many things when we were up in the air, and back on the ground we'd have as much or more to share about the flight we just completed, and our plans for the next one. Dad was, and always will be, my co-pilot. It was hard to accept that there would never be another takeoff with him. I could relate to the Cub itself: grounded, and in pieces. However, there was more turbulence to come.

In addition to the loss of my dad, my married life was troubled: in 1986, the kids and I moved into Mom's basement, and Bob and I divorced. Bob just didn't understand my passion for flying, or my strong affection for the Cub. Neither did my second husband, Steve Lang, to whom I was married from 1988 to 1997. I wanted to fly the Cub and maintain it, and I needed their help. Unless I had their support in this, as well as in our marriage overall, the personal chemistry just wouldn't work.

You might wonder how I can make such brief mention of two divorces; as anyone who has been through it knows, it can truly be a challenge. But nothing compares to the tragedy of the death of a loved one, particularly the death of a child. In 1988, while fishing with a friend on Devil Track Lake, my son, Laetham, drowned. I felt this loss deeply, and life became a blur for some time. One thing that gave me some solace was reading about airplanes and aviation. Flying had always been a hobby, but during this time it was a lifeline; it gave me a future to hope for.

John Gillespie Magee, Jr., an American fighter pilot who flew a British Spitfire with the Royal Canadian Air Force in WWII, offered one such light in the fog. He was killed at age 19 during a training flight. His poem is one of the best descriptions of the joy and freedom of flight:

"High Flight"

Oh! I have slipped the surly bonds of earth,
And danced the skies on laughter-silvered wings;
Sunward I've climbed, and joined the tumbling mirth
Of sun-split clouds,—and done a hundred things
You have not dreamed of—Wheeled and soared and swung
High in the sunlit silence. Hov'ring there
I've chased the shouting wind along, and flung
My eager craft through footless halls of air...
Up, up the long, delirious, burning blue
I've topped the wind-swept heights with easy grace
Where never lark or even eagle flew—
And, while with silent lifting mind I've trod
The high untrespassed sanctity of space,
Put out my hand, and touched the face of God.

CHAPTER 13:

Aloft Again

I felt the "surly bonds of earth" quite heavily some days. Though I moved on from Hedstrom's Lumber to work at the Grand Marais State Bank, which was easier on the body, money was tight. There were lots of conversations and worry, and at times I didn't know how I was going to pay my next bill. But through it all, like a shining hint of dawn on the horizon, was the dream I just couldn't give up, the desire that remained throughout every difficulty and heartbreak: I had to fly the Cub again.

Once you fly in a small plane, you enter a whole new realm of life's meaning. There's the adventure of leaving the security of the ground and embracing unknown winds, perhaps even turbulence. It's a means to find out what defines you, a challenge I craved. I wanted to once again hear the swoosh of water embracing the Cub's floats during take-off. I wanted to be engulfed by the sounds of the wind and the engine. I wanted to, from a great height, see clearly what was around me. I wanted to have some say in things, to do what I truly wanted to do. In flight, there is really no one else to push this aside. In short, I wanted to take control of my destiny. I just had to rebuild the Cub.

I had inherited the Cub after Dad's passing, and it was stored, in pieces, in a garage at my mother's house for 11 years. I worked and saved and scraped money together, and somehow, by the grace of God, I finally had enough. When, in 1992, good friend and fellow pilot, Russell Smith, asked if he could help with the restoration, I quickly agreed. He and Rodney Roy, manager of the Grand Marais airport and a nationally recognized expert in vintage aircraft restoration, got to work. The main wood spars in each wing were replaced, and the Cub was recovered with new fabric and repainted in the traditional yellow. My old friend was airworthy again.

The airport itself underwent a rebuild as well. Although its original location had the benefit of being adjacent to the seaplane base, airfield runway length and hangar space were limited. Because of high construction costs and limited available county land, it couldn't be expanded. So, in 1996 the airport was moved to its present site.

I was busy working full-time at the bank, and tending to a garden and animals on my rural property. I also became a foster parent; over the years I had a total of 33 foster children. Most were for just a night or two or three, but six children were with me for a year or more. One boy, Christian, stayed for about six years and is still very much a part of the family.

In early 1999, I needed a new septic system and I contacted Berneking Construction to see what could be done. Doug Finn was a partner in this firm. He was four years younger than me, and I remembered him as the cute little Finn boy at school. He had married, but was also divorced. He, too, had taken flying lessons when he was young, soloed while living up on the Iron Range, started a family, and then stopped flying. When he came out to check on the septic situation, we immediately connected and, as the saying goes, the rest is history. I had finally met someone who understood how much flying was a part of me. He once said, "When Kathy gets into the Cub, it's as natural for her as putting on her pants." Our romance blossomed, and we were married April 22, 2000, in a charming wedding. We were joined by my girls, who were grown and living in the Twin Cities; Doug's son, Jake; and the foster children I had at the time.

My life today is pretty full with gardening, a few chickens, and always a dog and a cat. There have always been other animals through the years like horses or goats, and you never know what will show up. I can rejoice with more time to pursue my interests, work and play with Doug, be with family and friends and, of course, fly the J-3 Cub.

The Cub has always been more than just a vehicle, more than a means to an end. It's a part of the family, a "living being;" something no other material possession can equal, laced with loving memories of my dad and our whole family. It truly shaped our lives, helping to build Skyport Lodge and put food on the table. My feelings for the Cub are almost human. It's like seeing a dear friend: you are overjoyed to meet them.

CHAPTER 14:

Hangar Flying

"[Flying is] a feeling of limitless freedom, of endless horizons, a grand adventure."

—Rinker Buck, *If We Had Wings*

In 2023, Cook County and the Grand Marais airport celebrates 75 years of aviation service to northeastern Minnesota and the Upper Midwest. I know Dad would be very pleased that his legacy continues, both at the beautiful new Skyport Lodge with its very capable young owners, and at the modernized Grand Marais airport.

Today, the airport boasts a newly extended 5,000-foot-long runway that can accommodate most jet and turbo-prop aircraft, especially the twin-engine "water bombers" used by the U.S. Forest Service, which formerly had to locate and refuel in Ely. Ensuring that the large Forest Service aircraft have a suitable and safe airstrip close to the Canadian border was a primary stimulus in the upgrade.

The airport features a newly remodeled flight center, office and visitor lounge, an automated weather station (AWOS), RNAV/GPS and NDB approaches when weather conditions hinder landings, ample parking space, heated hangars, and both gas and jet fuel. While the Grand Marais airport does not have a control tower, it does have access to a FAA Flight Service Station by Remote Communications Outlet (a radio signal that is routed by phone line), and Air Traffic Control Center for Instrument Flight Rules (IFR) flight. Rodney Roy, airport manager, and Roy Aero Service offers full-service aircraft maintenance, including float installation.

The airport commission board is focused on promoting the facilities for an increasing number of both private and corporate aircraft visits each year. Additional support also comes from many local pilots, plane owners, and enthusiasts dedicated to the promotion of general aviation in Cook County. It's clear that the importance and value of aviation has found a good home here, and continues to grow.*

Pilots are not required to log their flight hours, and I don't really know the exact number I've accumulated over the years—a confession that Dad wouldn't like as he was a stickler on good maintenance, and a log provides an informative timeline. But, my total overall flight time no doubt exceeds 350 hours, including training time flying with Dad. Now, in the autumn of my life, I can only wonder how many more years I will fly.

I've loved every minute of the Cub's presence in my life and its ability to transport me to distant realms of joy. And I know there will come a time when I will close the door on this period in my life. Piper Cub #N32955 will be passed on to either our family or someone else. Ginger's daughter and granddaughter have expressed interest in learning to fly. This is great news as it will be a wonderful opportunity to not only keep the Cub flying, but to keep our family's flying heritage alive as well.

I truly encourage not only our family members to fly, but for you, dear reader, wherever you are, to heed the call to touch the sky; to reach wonderful new heights of personal growth and awareness. Yes, the challenges and trials, both perceived and real, may hold you back. Yet, you've read my views up to this point, so you must realize that such challenges should not prevent you from chasing the wind. The thrill of flight is a dimension of life unlike any other.

No matter one's age or abilities, there is always an opening to a more invigorating and satisfying life, and that way, for me, was flight. Flying gave me self-confidence, courage, and the strength to test myself in new ways. I never felt I couldn't manage whatever was in front of me. A new situation or big job was never too much to handle. I am not saying I never failed at anything—I did—but it never stopped me from trying again. When you're up in the air in the Cub and all of a sudden you encounter some difficulty, you can't just get out of it. Like my dad modeled for me, I'd just change tactics a bit, adjust my attitude and approach, and charge on. There's an old sailor's saying that

---

*This information is partially excerpted from the files of the Cook County Historical Society, early issues of the *Cook County News Herald*, *Minnesota Flyer*, and *Northern Wilds Media*.

fits here: "You cannot change the wind, but you can assuredly change your sails."

Such an orientation in life tells me that young people, especially young women, should consider careers in aviation. We need all manner of capable pilots, and though this line of work was often associated with men in the past, there's no reason it should remain so.

For those who would rather keep their feet on the ground, the field of aviation welcomes critical skills in air frame and mechanical services, instruction, marketing and sales, research, and product design to name a few. Numerous college level aviation courses and ground schools attest to a growing marketplace.

And, no wonder! So much has changed in aviation over the years. Flying is an almost spiritual experience, a world of magic and awe that for centuries was only a dream for earth-bound humans who observed birds in flight and wondered what it would be like to fly as well. Now, in a limited manner, we know. While we don't have wings and feathers to fly, we do have our flying machines, some of which may soon take us into outer space as casually as we board a passenger plane today. No matter the type of aircraft or non-motorized form of human flight, the experience gives rise to all sorts of opportunities for self-growth and awareness, an open door to a fuller life.

I realize now that the joy of flying is more than just being up in the air. It also encompasses people from all walks of life who are connected to planes in some way. Ever hear of "hangar flying?" That's when pilots and friends sit in a hangar and chat about flight, planes, and aviation experiences over a cup of coffee. Regional fly-ins foster this, including our local Grand Marais event each fall, complete with a pancake breakfast. It's always a treat to visit with other like-minded folks.

Though I can't do a lot of the things I took for granted in years past, (and I may do more and more hangar flying as the years go on), I have no plans to give up the skies anytime soon. I don't hesitate to ask friends or other pilots to help me pull the Cub out of the hangar, to pull the prop smartly to start it, or whatever the task may be. Russell Smith and I flew together for several years, and nowadays his son, David, lends a hand with maintenance and flies it occasionally.

The open sky has made me feel free. It has offered me new horizons to pursue, and the Cub has been my trusty companion and compass of hope. Dad was right. Flying gets into your blood.

The sky is the limit and it's waiting for you now. As Amelia Earhart once said: "No borders, just horizons—only freedom."

I hope for you all the joys of flight.

With appreciation and affection,

—Kathryn Krotz-Finn

EPILOGUE

Chasing the North Wind

There is a source of energy moving through my hands as I lightly grip the familiar control stick. Alert to any wind gusts that may suddenly buffet the Cub, I let the plane rise or fall, roll left or right under control, just to feel its nature and to be part of it and the wind. I am at one with my ship, dancing on currents of unknown origins, and I'm free with the sky. It's all of this, and more.

Life in the upper Cook County area is not always easy. Outside of seasonal residents or visitors, those who live and work here year-round are always busy carving out a living however they can. As I fly, I look at small farms or remote homesteads, lakeside lodges, and cabins of all descriptions. I follow old forest roads, check to see whose fields or livestock are in good shape, and who may be out cutting wood for the next winter season.

Beautiful Lake Superior has its moods and there is always something to see or follow along its rocky shore, too. Highway 61, Minnesota's North Shore drive that stretches from Duluth to the Canadian border, offers another visual treat, a highway that will soon be extra busy with the annual spring influx of fishermen and tourists fleeing their distant urban homes.

During these flights it is not unusual to find someone looking up at me, so I'll wag my wings to say 'hello' and sometimes these good folks wave back. It's hard to miss a slow-moving yellow Cub against a clear blue sky. During fishing season, friends sometimes have asked me to land on the lake where they're fishing, as they feel this helps the fish bite. I'm not sure this ever did make a difference. Yet, in this simple manner I am connected with the north country community.

When I'm aloft, I try to not think too much about the demands of family, home, or community obligations. I've never overly concentrated on the technical side of things like Dad did. But then, I haven't had to use the Cub to feed my family. To be flying is to experience a welcome release from all that ties me to the ground. Now, I am one with the wind, and my yellow charger carries me easily toward the western horizon of our vast boreal forest clothed in aspen, red and white pine, birch trees, and maples; timeless hallmarks of our northland home. The southwest wind remains steady as I fly west, following a random course tracking to one lake, then another. There is always the urge to follow an unseen line leading me along to the ever-beckoning distant horizon, yet I'm reminded of the limitations of time, fuel, and places to land should in-flight trouble occur.

During my rambling cross-country flights, I occasionally pass over many acres of forest damaged by wind or destroyed by past fires, a reminder of the ever-present dangers we try to monitor year-round. While light green foliage of the prolific aspens and maples is now returning, it will take many years for the majestic pine and spruce to return to their full canopy and wilderness beauty in the Superior National Forest. Nature can heal here, but perhaps not fully in my lifetime.

Over the course of an hour or so, I continue to see a few birds flying below me. It won't be long before I encounter more and more migrating birds, especially many kinds of ducks and geese. Their traditional 'v' formations are a pleasure to see and a reminder of another good season ahead. I wish I could follow them to their northern destinations, their migratory urge pulling them back once again to their summer ranges further north. All I can do now is wag my wings, give them the right of way, and wish them a safe journey.

While the Cub has a flying time of approximately two hours on a full tank, actual flight time will always depend on the vagaries of strong headwinds, crosswinds, or tailwinds and, occasionally, pilot fatigue. It's wise to not continue unnecessarily with low fuel, and I've been up now for almost two hours so reluctantly, I gently move the control stick to my left along with slight foot pressure on the left rudder pedal and slowly bank and turn the Cub 180 degrees. The Cub responds easily to my touch and I feel the southwest wind gently lifting my right wing. From this point I follow Lake Superior's rock-studded shoreline east until I see the sun's reflections on the 7-mile, east-west surface of Devil Track Lake. The sun's warm light covers the lake's surface, creating shiny diamonds on myriad small waves, a most pleasant sight from my lofty perch.

I know I still have enough fuel to check on a few small area lakes to see how much ice they still hold, and, sure enough, several lakes still have some, now dull in color as the sun works its magic on winter's remains. This is yet another reminder that spring arrives slowly in the north.

As I return to Devil Track Lake, I check for the direction of the waves, the ripples of wind on the water, or any movement of the tree tops. There is still a slight southwest wind, and as I slowly descend and circle for my base run, I scan the lake to see if other planes or fishermen are present. Nothing appears out of order so I proceed on my base leg, reduce engine speed, make a slow turn to my left, and begin my final descent. Sunshine fills the cockpit and I listen to the soft smooth purring of the slowing engine.

As I continue my descent, I want to be performing at my best as it's easier on the Cub and on my ego. After all, as the only apparent registered female Cub pilot in Cook County, I have a reputation to uphold. Landing speed is around 58 mph with wings level. When both floats first skim the lake's surface, I maintain enough power to keep smooth forward momentum before I reduce power gradually and allow the floats to settle into the lake's surface. Then I maneuver the Cub to bring me back to the dock I had left two hours prior.

Once at the dock, I shut down the engine, climb out of the cockpit and onto the float, and stand there several minutes while looking up at the blue sky to reflect on my first spring flight. I feel a powerful sense of satisfaction and joy. I am at ease and I feel refreshed and excited about the coming months to fly in this beautiful country. The north air never smelled sweeter.

Not a bad run for this 73-year-old pilot.

POSTSCRIPT

Today, the old Skyport runway lies abandoned, but not empty. Deer have returned to feed on the grasses growing wherever the blacktop surface has given way. Birds and animals freely roam on this now open corridor where planes of all descriptions once came and went, and the silence is no longer broken by the noise of engines gaining speed or the screech of tires touching down. No small hangars exist anymore where several once stood, and the trusted old orange windsock is now only a distant memory.

Although an officially decommissioned airport, Skyport's history remains as a testament to the vision not only of the Krotz family, but to so many pilots and others over the years who followed and built the present airport that continues to add to Cook County's growing aviation story, a Minnesota legacy worth remembering.

An Invitation for Women Pilots

"Flying is totally my time...
the cares and burdens of being at home are no longer
things to distract me from my horizon ahead..."

—Beryl Markham

Women have made their mark, and made it early in the aviation community. In 1929, 20 brave women pilots embarked on the first all-female air race across several states in basic propeller-driven airplanes. Their heroic story is beautifully documented in the book *Sky Girls,* written by Gene Nora Jessen.

During WWII there were more than 1,000 volunteer female pilots who were flying each day for the ferrying command of the army, air force, and navy as Women Air Force Service Pilots (WASPs). In 1977, thanks to efforts led by WASP member Bernice "Bee" Falk Haydu, these pilots finally secured congressional acknowledgement and were officially recognized as WWII veterans. Bee said, "I'm proud of what we did. I'm proud that we showed the world that an airplane knows no sex. It doesn't know whether a monkey is flying it, or a man, or a woman, or what—it's your ability."

Another military pilot, Rosemary Mariner, became one of the U.S. Navy's first female pilots and the first woman to command a naval aviation squadron. She later successfully fought for a congressional measure that lifted a ban on women serving in combat.

The field of aviation for women is growing. So, whatever your station in life or your age, every person can and should have the chance to explore new paths before it's too late. Don't be afraid to do this. I've had some personal challenges but I chose to keep going, and I'm glad I did. As Anne Morrow Lindbergh once said, "It takes as much courage to have tried and failed as it does to have tried and succeeded." Beryl Markham said, "In the air no horizon is so far that you cannot get above it or beyond it."

The stage has been set by so many great aviators: Anne Morrow Lindbergh, Amelia Earhart, Blanche Stuart Scott (the first woman on record to solo a plane), Ruth Law, Bessie Coleman (the first African American woman pilot), Jackie Cochran, and Beryl Markham (famous even before she had crossed the Atlantic the hard way, going west against the wind). I strongly recommend the freedom that flying brings, for women in particular. We can so often get sidetracked helping our family and others, and our personal time slips by.

I recommend looking into The Ninety Nines, an international organization of women pilots established in 1929. Its first president was Amelia Earhart, and it's still active today. It has 19 chapters in nine states, including Minnesota. Another growing organization for female pilots is Women in Aviation International.

Adolescent fliers can get involved through KidsFlyCubs, a 501(c)(3) public charity via the American Legend Aircraft Company, dedicated to educating America's youth by providing free-of-charge high-quality stick-and-rudder-based flight training experiences for 15- to 17-year-olds involved in school or community-based aviation organizations. KidsFlyCubs is located in Flagler Beach, Florida.

So, have courage. Get above—and beyond—the horizon!

AIRCRAFT & AVIATION TERMS
Piper J-3 Cub

Ailerons: Long movable panels on the wings to aid in controlling the plane's banking angle.

Airspeed Indicator: Shows how fast you are going through the air (not in relation to the ground).

Altimeter: Measures your altitude above sea level.

Control Stick: Vertical metal stick connected to cables beneath the floor that move the plane's elevator, rudder, and ailerons. This stick is located between the pilot's legs and is used to control all aspects of the plane's movements. The J-3 Cub has two control sticks for the tandem seating arrangement to aid in flight instruction or flying from the rear seat. Most modern light planes have yokes (similar to a car's steering wheel, but smaller).

Elevator: Horizontal tail assembly that moves up and down to direct the up or down attitude of the plane.

Fixed Base of Operations (FBO): Airport that includes aviation fuel, mechanical services, pilot information, landing instructions, pilot training, and rest facilities.

Flaps: Movable wing panels, positioned between the outer ailerons and the plane's body, that control the amount of lift. This mechanism enables a slower descent and faster take-offs from short airfields.

Instrument Flight Rating (IFR): Special training and qualification allowing a pilot to fly in most weather conditions when their plane is adequately equipped with standard flight instruments for this purpose. Relies on the pilot's abilities to use the appropriate instruments available in the plane, and briefings and weather information provided by Federal Aviation Administration weather stations.

Magnetos: Two electrical generators that provide spark to spark plugs in each cylinder to start and run the engine. When the engine is running at start-up, one magneto at a time is closed and should show only a slight drop in rpms.

Pitot Tube: Tube-like nozzle that measures the velocity (air speed) of the plane through the air.

Pre-Flight Inspection: Series of inspection steps done before starting the engine, to ensure the plane is airworthy.

Rudder: Large vertical tail used to turn the plane via the rudder pedals for either right or left turns.

Stall: Reaction of the plane in nose-high attitude where air flow is slowed over the wings and not enough lift is available to keep the plane aloft. In a stall, the plane literally stops flying until the pilot puts the plane's nose down and advances power to regain lift and level or controlled flight.

Tachometer: Instrument that shows engine rpms.

Throttle: Mechanism to control amount of fuel supplied to the engine, thus the rpms.

Turbo Prop: Modern high-speed/performance engine that provides greater power to the plane.

Visual Flight Rules (VFR): Flying by sight in clear weather, with minimum reliance on instruments.

PROFILE OF
Clarence J. Krotz

Military Service:
- Began active military service with the U.S. Army Air Corps, May 24, 1943
- Saw action in Sardinia, Italy, North Africa, and the European Theater
- Trained asa B-26 Lockheed Martin Marauder bomber pilot
- Member of the 432nd Bomber Squadron, Mediterranean Theater of Operations covering North Africa and Italy
- Completed 73 missions; served two tours of duty
- Nearly killed on last mission when a canon shell came through the plane's nose, killing his co-pilot
- Awarded two Bronze Stars, EAME Campaign Medal, Presidential Unit Citation with one Oak Leaf Cluster, and the Air Medal with five Oak Leaf Clusters
- Discharged from active-duty October 7, 1945; Age: 25
- Rank: First Lieutenant

Civilian Aviation:
- Arrived in Cook County in 1945
- Purchased Bent's Resort on 77 acres with savings from his military service
- Began construction on the airport and finished the 2,150-foot-long sod strip in 1947
- Skyport airport received its official operating license in October 1947
- Krotz was featured in the April 2, 1948 issue of the *Cook County News Herald* article, "Who's Who in North Shore Aviation"
- Skyport airport was designated the official Grand Marais airport, November 1948
- Skyport airport received official certificate/license of approval September 27, 1952, MN State Department of Aeronautics
- Skyport airport incorporated in June 1954

- Received his Federal Airman's Certificate of Competency and ratings in S&MEL, SES, Flight Instructor, Helicopter CAA #234541 Commercial, May 10, 1955
- Served as manager of the airport until 1965
- Granted license by the Air Transport Board, Ottawa, Canada, for a Class 9-4 International non-scheduled charter-commercial air service to transport persons and goods from a base at Grand Marais, MN, USA, to points in the Province of Ontario, Canada. August 1967
- Received Skyport Lodge Seaplane Base, Public Airport License #1474, January 11, 1972, from State of Minnesota Department of Aeronautics
- Sold his aviation business in 1980 after devoting nearly 35 years of his life in the development and promotion of aviation in Cook County
- Served as a member of the Cook County airport board for many years
- Died May 30, 1981 (61 years old)
- Skyport airport dedicated as the Clarence Krotz Memorial Airport, October 1982

History of the Grand Marais Airport

Adapted from the History of the Grand Marais Airport, *by Olga Soderberg, president of the Cook County Historical Society, and as provided by Clarence J. Krotz.*

In October of 1945, Clarence Krotz arrived in Cook County ready to pursue his dream. With his brothers Frank and Lon, he formed a company called Skyport Lodge. He then purchased Bent's Resort to develop his own lodge. Gaining financial support through the Grand Marais State Bank, he began the development in an area that presented almost unlimited potential bringing in tourists to the resort by feeder line and distributing them by seaplane to wilderness lakes and camps.

This was true pioneering work to develop the layout and engineering of the airport, clearing the forest with heavy earth-moving bulldozers. Rough grading, rock picking, and finish grading was then completed with a second-hand grader and home-built cement rollers. These were pulled by surplus army trucks. Much of the equipment and the first windsock were made by Al Bally. All the construction was completed on the new 2,150-foot sod strip in the two years between October 1945 and October 1947, when Clarence was issued the first airport license for the site by the State Aeronautics Department. Up to this point, all money spent on the project were the private funds of Skyport Lodge.

In this period, the main lodge building was built and the existing structures modernized. The lodge operation was managed by Mr. and Mrs. H. Hadaway, Krotz's mother and stepfather. The airport also figured in the non-flying recreational development of the county. Krotz and others organized the first official skiing in Cook County along with a winter carnival day. They reorganized the dormant Fisherman's

Picnic and reactivated it as a yearly event. During these immediate post war years, they reactivated the Fourth of July celebration which was held in part at Skyport Lodge. Other public activities included airshows by the Cole Brothers Flying Circus, Summer Sports Day Events, and fly-ins.

In the early 1950s, the Wilderness Area came into effect and Skyport Lodge became an official aircraft check-in point for this area, until the area was closed to all flying. The airport was later sold to the state, which in turn enlarged it to 2,800 feet and made it a municipal airport and seaplane base. Krotz kept Skyport Lodge and Resort and accepted a non-paying job as manager of the airport, a capacity he held until 1965 when the state turned the airport over to the county.

The runway remained turf until the county blacktopped it and installed an instrument apparatus approach and flight service phone. In 1965, the county also established an airport commission, which sponsored and installed a UNICOM radio, weather station, summertime customs station, and obtained federal funds to help in the improvements to the airstrip.

Floats or Wheels

September 4, 1980, *Cook County News Herald*

Whether You've Got Floats or Wheels, Devil Track Airport Could Be For You—"A gem in the wilderness," "A really important asset to the county," "A necessity," "A showcase for aviation tourists," are all comments from area people, summer residents and pilots that use Devil Track Airport.

The airport, sitting high on Maple Hill, is readily seen from the air because of its landmark, Devil Track Lake. The lake has always provided a scenic and useful asset to the airport since it first got its license in October 1947. Part of an exceptional quality the airport possesses, is the fact that it affords accessibility by float planes, which makes it one of few of its kind in the nation.

Before the county resurfaced the airstrip, the airport was only on visual flight rules (VFR) status. Later, when the instrument approach was installed, pilots could fly according to flight center instructions when weather demanded it and they had an IFR (instrument flight) rating.

A great variety of planes have utilized the strip over the years. From a vintage bi-plane to the recent first landing of a Cessna Citation jet, the small airport has provided an adequate safe facility for landing. According to Clarence Krotz, founder, developer and long time proprietor of the airport, "There has never been an accident attributable to the airport itself."

The seaplane access affords an opportunity for businessmen as well as the recreational flyer. When the weather conditions are not favorable on the Grand Marais harbor, float planes must land at Devil Track. In 1964 and 1965, Ford tri-motors and TBM bombers were flown in and out of the airport spraying for the Spruce Budworm for the US Forest Service.

The National Park Service has used Skyport airfield for business purposes and the North American Life and Casualty has used it extensively for their guests. They have turbo prop planes. One of the largest planes to land at the Devil Track site was a Martin 404, which has a capacity of approximately 50 passengers. Helicopters have also used the airstrip. "We can handle over 95 percent of the aircraft now," said Clarence Krotz.

"It's really important for our remote area to have an airport for the safety and welfare of all of the county and for future business. It's an asset to have this airport and it will become more and more important in the future," says Roger Vanderzee, a local pilot.

AIRPORT STATISTICS 1947-1965

Statistics from the first license in 1947 as an airport, to 1965 when the county took over:
- Approximately 140 transient landings per summer season
- Largest aircraft to land: DC-3
- Oldest pilot: Joe Reads, pilot license #61
- The first plane to land on the airstrip was from the Arrowhead Flying Club in Duluth
- Average aviation gas to transient aircraft: 1,700 gallons per season
- Number of aircraft accidents involving damage or injuries: None
- Cost of airport operations to county 1947 to 1965: None

COOK COUNTY AVIATION QUIZ

1. When was the first official Cook County/ Grand Marais airport established?
2. Who built the first official Grand Marais airport?
3. What famous airplane was used to transport people and goods around our region from this airport and is still operational today as the only registered craft of its type still flying in Cook County?
4. What large aircraft, that featured corrugated metal side covering, used the Grand Marais airport?
5. What year did construction first begin on the original Grand Marais airport?
6. Where was the original airport located?
7. What was the name of the first official Grand Marais airport?
8. In what year was the airport relocated uphill to its present site?
9. What were the main reasons this change occurred?
10. Which daughter of the original airport family ultimately got her pilot's license and is still flying today?
11. Who is the individual nationally recognized as a leader in vintage aircraft restoration working at the Grand Marais airport?
12. What was the primary reason the new airport main runway was extended to 5,002 feet?
13. When was the first airplane purchased in Cook County?

Answers:

1. November 11, 1948
2. Clarence J. Krotz
3. Piper J-3 Cub
4. Ford Tri-Motor Transport
5. December 20, 1933
6. On the present site of the Grand Marais high school
7. Clarence Krotz Memorial Airport
8. 1996
9. Lack of additional land to expand, insufficient runway length to accommodate large aircraft, limited space for hangars, parking space, storage, etc.
10. Kathryn Krotz-Finn
11. Rodney Roy, owner of Roy Aero Service; manager of the Grand Marais airport
12. To accommodate larger aircraft, including DNR water bombers to fight forest fires
13. August, 1928, a hydroplane purchased by Frank and Will Powell of Gunflint Lake

TIMELINE

1900s   Tourism grows on the North Shore

1913   Benoit XIV No. 43 bi-plane 'flying boat' shipped to Duluth

1919   U.S. Army to fight fires with planes

1920   Clarence Krotz born in Chicago (May 16)

1921   U.S. Air Congress to be formed (November)

1928   Frank and Will Powell (Gunflint Lake) buy hydroplane

1929   Aircraft arrived with guests at Gateway (Naniboujou) Lodge (winter)

300 locals ride in the Tri-Motor Ford plane on Grand Marais harbor ice

1930   Plane from Ely used for fire patrol (September)

1931   Ryan five-passenger monoplane added to assist firefighting; based in Tower, MN

Greenwood Lake resident planned to buy five-passenger plane for regular service from Duluth to Grand Marais and Gunflint Trail

1932   Formation of emergency air scout patrol (Canadian border)

1933   WPA support for Grand Marais airport; construction begins (December 20)

1936   Grand Marais airstrip doesn't pass inspection (July 23)

1940s   Former sheriff Emerson Morris buys a plane, as do others

Bob Blackwell and Paul Sjobergh start a business to service Isle Royale from Grand Marais; the business folds

1943   Clarence Krotz begins active military service (May 24)

1945   Clarence Krotz is discharged and arrives in Cook County, forms company called Skyport Lodge with brothers Frank and Lon (October)

Grading/construction of sod landing strip begins at Skyport

1946 Clarence Krotz buys Devil Track Lodge (August 15)

Clarence Krotz marries Dorothy Rindahl

1947 Ginger Krotz is born (January 27)

First commercial service offered via Seabee between Grand Marais and Isle Royale (September)

Construction finishes at Skyport (October)

1948 Kathy Krotz is born (June 10)

Clarence Krotz featured in "Who's Who" of Cook County aviation

Skyport airport licensed (October)

Grand Marais field given limited license

State informs Krotz family that Skyport may only be private; offers $10,000 buyout

Skyport becomes the official Cook County airstrip (November 11)

1949 Aircraft wilderness ban passes, starting January 1951; 1952 for routes in use

Clarice Krotz is born (December 17)

1950 Krotz family purchases 1941 Piper J-3 Cub (final year of manufacturing the Cub)

1951 Wilderness plane ban in effect except private holdings served by plane (January)

1952 Wilderness plane ban fully in effect (January)

1954 Skyport airport incorporated (June)

1959 Tri-Pacer purchased

1964 Kathy's first solo flight (July 31)

1965 Skyport airfield sold to state for $10,000; state then deeded to county for $1

UNICOM radio installed, weather station, summer customs station, airstrip improved (Kathy is the first to operate UNICOM system)

Clarence Krotz retires from managing Skyport airport

1970 Kathy marries Robert Sopoci

Daughter Lieschen is born (September 20)

1972 Skyport seaplane base receives public airport license (January 11)

Son Laetham is born (September 9)

1973 Daughter Steina is born (July 18)

TIMELINE | 91

1979 Kathy takes flight lessons at Crystal airport and earns her pilot's license

1980 Kathy, Bob, and kids move to Grand Marais permanently

Clarence and Dorothy Krotz sell Skyport Lodge

Clarence Krotz retires from volunteering to manage airport

1981 Clarence Krotz dies (May 30)

Kathy inherits J-3 Cub

1982 Dedication ceremony for "Clarence Krotz Memorial Airfield"

1986 Divorces Bob Sopoci

1988 Laetham drowns

Kathy marries Steve Lang

1992 J-3 Cub restored

1996 Airport expands and moves to present site

1997 Kathy divorces Steve Lang

2000 Kathy marries Doug Finn

2011 Dorothy Krotz dies (October 14)

2023 75-year anniversary of aviation in Cook County

SELECTED BIBLIOGRAPHY

American Legend Aircraft Company, 1810 Piper Lane, Sulphur Springs, TX 75482

Minnesota Flyer Newsletter, July 1, 2017, "Airport of the Month," Grand Marais/Cook County Airport

Cook County Historical Society Archives, Grand Marais, Minnesota

Cook County Library, Microfilm copies of Grand Marais News Herald Newspapers, 1919 to present

A Gift of Wings, Richard Bach, 1974, Bantam Doubleday Dell Publishing Group, Inc., 666 Fifth Avenue, New York, NY 10103

Bush Pilots, Bob Cary and Jack Hautala, 2003, Adventure Publications, Inc., 820, Cleveland Street South, Cambridge, MN 55008

Alaska's Bush Planes, Ned Rozell, 2004, Alaska Northwest Books, Graphic Arts Center Publishing Co., P. O. Box 10306, Portland, OR 97296-0306

Flight of Passage, Rinker Buck, 1997, Hyperion, 114 Fith Avenue, New York, NY 10011

If We Had Wings, The Enduring Dream of Flight, Rinker Buck, 2001, Crown Publishers, New York, NY

Piper's Golden Age, Alan Abel, Drina Welch Abel and Paul Matt, 2001, Wind Canyon Books, P. O. Box 511, Brawley, CA 92227

B-26 Marauder Units in the MTO, Mark Styling, 2008, Osprey Publishing Midland House, West Way, Botley, Oxford, OX2 OPH, 443 Park Avenue South, New York, NY 10016

Northern Wilds Media, Elle Andra-Warner, September 2017, Northern Wilds Publications, Grand Marais, MN 55604

KidsFlyCubs.org, Flagler Beach, Florida

V – Mail, "The Accidental Pilot," Vol. 36, No. 4 Winter 2018, The National WWII Museum, 945 Magazine Street, New Orleans, LA 70130

Gene Glader, Ph.D., author, History of Grand Marais, MN; Cascade Lodge

PROFILES

Kathryn Krotz-Finn

A proud native of Cook County, Kathy *(pictured on the right with Doug Finn)* was born into aviation. Her father, Clarence J. Krotz, a former WWII bomber pilot, built his own northwoods lodge, airport, and seaplane base on Devil Track Lake in northeastern Minnesota. Kathryn's mother, Dorothy, was equally talented and with three small girls to raise and a lodge and airport to help run, she and the girls formed a tight knit team that helped usher aviation into Minnesota's remote Arrowhead region. Whether sitting behind her father while he flew the vintage 1941 Piper J-3 Cub, or piloting the Cub by herself today, flying became and remains an important part of Kathryn's life. Today, she owns the Cub and enjoys flying around the Arrowhead region as often as she can. Kathryn and her husband, Doug, live on a small 15-acre rural homestead in Cook County near Grand Marais.

Richard C. Struck

Richard's lifelong fascination with small planes began when he made model planes as a child. Although never a pilot or plane owner, this interest continued throughout his professional 34-year career in public relations and philanthropy. Whenever possible, he logged many hours of flying both for pleasure and work in small aircraft. Richard *(pictured on the left with David Smith)* is retired and lives in southern Minnesota with his wife, Peggy.

Wolfgang Greiner

Pilot, airplane owner, and resident of Cook County, Wolfgang appreciates the magic of flight and the lasting impact that the Krotz family has had on aviation in the Arrowhead region of Minnesota. He lives on the shores of Devil Track Lake where the Krotz family story began.

Printed in the USA
CPSIA information can be obtained
at www.ICGtesting.com
CBHW052323051223
2393CB00003B/6